Donna Gustin, MN, RN B
St. Joseph Hosp.-So. Campus
809 E. Chestnut Street
Bellingham, WA 98225

HEALTH, HEALING & WHOLENESS

HEALTH, HEALING & WHOLENESS

ENGAGING CONGREGATIONS IN MINISTRIES OF HEALTH

Mary Chase-Ziolek

THE PILGRIM PRESS   CLEVELAND

The Pilgrim Press, 700 Prospect Avenue, Cleveland, Ohio 44115-1100
thepilgrimpress.com

Printed in the United States of America on acid-free paper

10   09   08   07   06   05   5   4   3   2   1

Library of Congress Cataloging-in-Publication Data

Chase-Ziolek, Mary, 1952–
    Health, healing & wholeness : engaging congregations in
    ministries of health / Mary Chase-Ziolek.
        p.   cm.
    Includes bibliographical references (p.).
    ISBN 0-8298-1652-6 (paperback. : alk. paper)
    1. Church work with the sick.   I. Title: Health, healing, and
wholeness.   II. Title.

BV4335.C465   2005
261.8'321–dc22

                                        2004060229

CONTENTS

FOREWORD

Congregations have always been places where we bring our deepest needs and longings for wholeness. In fact, the connection between faith and health runs deep in all religious traditions. In the early church, care of the sick and the marginalized was a central function. The writings of Maimonides, a twelfth-century Jewish doctor and philosopher, explored profound faith and health links. The health care system that I work for was founded over a hundred years ago by people in Christian congregations who saw health needs in their communities and responded by building hospitals, training nurses, and serving troubled youth.

What we do in congregations changes lives and transforms communities. Care, nurture, and healing have always been part of religious life, but increasingly congregations are building intentional ministries that reflect the connection.

This book is a wonderful introduction to the health ministry movement—and a movement it is. The field is wide open and growing. There is no one way to do health ministry and there is still much to learn about how churches, synagogues, temples, and mosques can live out this calling. This rich potential is both the beauty and the challenge of health ministry. It can be hard not to feel overwhelmed by all that we are called to as people of faith. This book helps frame the work by offering historical and biblical perspective, providing practical approaches and steps, and demonstrating a range of ways that congregations are expressing this ministry.

Chase-Ziolek also calls us to take seriously the full extent of what faith communities can offer. She highlights key biblical themes in healing–right relationship, justice, restoration to community, *nephesh* or the unity of body and soul, shalom, salvation, and health as a process. These are powerful, transforming principles. What if we really lived them out? Could we actually impact the infant mortality rates of our communities? Could we actually help people to live better longer? Could we eliminate the health disparities that plague the poor? What if we really believed that our gathering, our worship, our caring for each other, our commitment to justice and abundant life for all makes a difference? What if we lived as though the church was a place of healing for each other and our communities?

It's really not that complicated. Gary Gunderson, director of the Interfaith Health Program at Emory University in Atlanta, is one of my mentors. He notes that

> The cutting edge of health ministry does not lie up some unexplored river, over some academic horizon, in some clever new management paradigm, out amid some cosmic mystery. The cutting edge is in between us, among those who literally share our breath and water, our food and shelter. The cutting edge of health ministries is not technical but relational . . . how we care for each other.

As you read this book, I encourage you to delve into your own congregation's history of healing ministry and imagine what could happen as you claim this amazing tradition and live in the potential of what your congregation can do to transform each other and the world around you.

Rev. Kirsten Peachey, director
Congregational Health Partnerships
Advocate Health Care, Chicago, IL

PREFACE AND ACKNOWLEDGEMENTS

If ever there was a time to consider the possibilities for engaging congregations in ministries of health, that time is now. Societal trends in health care and our growing understanding of the dynamics of well-being have created an environment that cries out for the church to take on the challenge of health. The hard work of many individuals and organizations has prepared the soil. Ministries of health have sprung forth in congregations around the country and there is the possibility of an even greater harvest as churches live up to their potential of promoting health and wholeness.

The faith and health ministries movement began with a few fledgling groups in the 1980s working primarily with the models of parish nursing and lay health educators. Over time it has grown to embrace diverse health ministry approaches, and expanded to include community-based faith and health partnerships, as well as government initiatives to collaborate with the religious community. The supporting infrastructure has evolved, as have programs. Many of the early health ministry programs were started by hospitals whose support has ebbed and flowed over time. Denominational support for health ministries has grown, including opportunities for credentialing. Over time, an increasingly diverse group of individuals and organizations has been drawn to this work of reclaiming the church's role in health and healing.

In the past few months, I have attended three very different conferences, each centered on health ministries: the Health Ministries Association (HMA) conference in Seattle, a program of the Institute for Public Health and Faith Collaboration in Wisconsin, and the Westberg Symposium for parish nursing in St. Louis. Each of these meetings represents a health ministries theme. HMA reflects the interdisciplinary nature of this work. As a membership association, it brings together parish nurses, health educators, various therapists, other health professionals, and clergy to consider the work of helping congregations realize their potential to promote health. The Institute for Public Health and Faith Collaboration, a program of the Interfaith Health Program of Emory University, reflects the public health perspective of this work that looks at the big picture and the potential of congregations of any faith to work in partnerships to improve the health of their communities. The Westberg Symposium reflects the significant part nursing has played in the development of health ministries as the parish nursing role has grown. Nurses and churches have been drawn to the parish nursing model, yet it is the broader concept of health ministry that informs the practice of parish nursing, as well as that of other health ministers. Woven together, these strands have helped shape the backbone of the faith and health movement as congregations have been challenged to consider how essential promoting health is to their mission. A separate but interrelated thread has been the growing interest in religion, spirituality, and health that has nurtured a climate conducive to the web of connection between faith and health.

Since 1991, I have had the privilege to serve in health ministries practice, administration, education, and research. I have served as the coordinator of Geriatric Health Ministry at Northwestern Memorial Hospital, working with a diverse, multiethnic group of churches and synagogues, and most recently, as the director of the Center for Faith and Health at North Park Theological Seminary.

My hospital position was a community outreach effort. It was through this experience and particularly working with synagogues and African American churches that I came to appreciate the significance of congregational culture in shaping health ministries. While hospital sponsorship of that program discontinued several years after I left, many of those congregations have continued their ministries of health.

My current position as a nurse on a seminary faculty, teaching interdisciplinary classes in faith and health, reflects the need to prepare both health professionals and clergy to integrate faith and health in their practice settings and lead congregations in ministries of health. When the time comes that a pastor is just as likely to initiate health ministries as a health professional, we will know that health and healing are truly being integrated into the culture of our congregations.

There is a difference between how health ministry might best be expressed in an African American Baptist church on the south side of Chicago and a German Lutheran church on the north side of Chicago. There is a significant difference in how health ministry might best be expressed through a small Catholic church in rural Appalachia and how it might best be expressed in a large Evangelical Covenant Church in suburban California. The frequency of gathering, cultural values of ethnic groups, neighborhood issues, style of clergy leadership, and size of the congregation will all influence a church's ministry of health. There is no cookie cutter approach that fits all congregations. What does fit all congregations is an understanding of how each group has a unique culture with distinctive values and beliefs that will lead to a unique expression of health ministries.

Congregations may be motivated to engage in ministries of health to continue the tradition of Jesus' healing ministry, to address issues of injustice, relieve suffering, and nurture personal stewardship of one's body. There may also be practical or political motivations as well, such as providing members an opportunity to explore new areas of ministry or connecting to community organizations. It is my hope that this book will challenge churches to see the importance of reaching beyond their walls to improve the health of their communities. We experience health as individuals, but that experience is shaped by our community context. As churches engage in acts of compassion, mercy, and justice in service to their neighbors, it is ultimately the acts of justice that will move us towards health for all.

I am also aware of the inherently interdisciplinary nature of blending health and ministry. All kinds of health professionals, clergy, and interested lay people are needed in order for health ministries to reach their full potential. Consequently, my writing is intended for people from diverse health and ministry backgrounds.

This book is the result of a long journey on which there have been many companions. Throughout this journey there have been significant individuals whose lives and thoughts have interwoven with mine. There are two people I consider mentors in this field: Mary Ann McDemott, who served as my dissertation advisor and has remained a valued colleague and friend, and Tom Droege, whose writing first articulated for me the meaning of health ministries.

Throughout this book both implicit and explicit stories are interwoven. For the implicit stories I am indebted to all of the congregations and individuals with which I have had the privilege of working, and all of the students with whom I have had the privilege of learning. The explicit stories come from three students, Joan Scarborough, Carol Vos, and Pat Nafzger, and a colleague, Lois Augustson. Throughout my work in health ministries, I have been touched by the willingness of people to share their stories and their resources. Whether I have been writing or working in the field, my experience of health ministry has always been a collaborative effort.

I have had the privilege in my position at North Park Theological Seminary to work with a fine group of colleagues who have helped me develop the interdisciplinary nature of health ministries, including John Weborg, Jim Bruckner, Richard Carlson, Phillis Sheppard, Joan Zetterlund, and the late Burton Nelson. Their willingness to explore issues of faith and health in their respective fields and the willingness of our seminary leaders Stephen Graham and Jay Phelan to support this exploration has made our seminary uniquely positioned to cultivate interdisciplinary dialogue that can transform local churches' ministries of health. I am also indebted to the seminary and its board for the gift of sabbatical time for writing. This book emerged from an online class that has given me the opportunity to learn with students from around the country and given me the joy of seeing these concepts successfully applied in a wide range of settings.

The editorial support of Kim Martin Sadler has been invaluable in creating this text, as have the insights of Rev. Kirsten Peachey and Sally Johnson.

My family, including my husband, Keith, and children, Andrew and Emily, have been a steady source of support and encouragement. And I cannot forget those now gone, most particularly my father, Rev. James Chase, who implicitly taught me the connection between faith and health long before the term health ministries was coined.

1

A CONCEPTUAL FRAMEWORK FOR ENGAGING CONGREGATIONS IN MINISTRIES OF HEALTH

We live in an exciting time when congregations and health care organizations, clergy and health professionals are joining together to explore the possibilities of ministries of health. The growing national interest in the integration of faith and health is taking many different forms— from parish nurses to lay health promoters, from healing services to spiritual interventions in health care, from personal faith to medical research, from the lives of individuals to the lives of communities. One consequence of this renewed interest in the interrelationship between faith and health has been a positive influence on the health of individuals, families, and communities.

We are seeing congregations with parish nurses, health ministers, or lay health promoters working to enhance the well-being of their congregation. We are seeing congregations reaching out to their communities in ministry with persons with AIDS or working with immigrant groups to improve their health. We are seeing congregations recognizing a need for health services among the uninsured in their community and creating faith-based health clinics. Around the country we are seeing the potential for effective faith and health partnerships that can change the life of communities as congregations and hospitals, departments of health, home health agencies, departments on aging, and social service agencies work together on health issues of mutual concern. These faith and health partnerships that would not even have been considered thirty years ago are now seen as essential to improving the health of our communities. Truly we are in the midst of a faith and health movement urging congregations and health care institutions, clergy and health professionals, to move forward to new possibilities.

Within the faith and health movement, the majority of congregations involved in congregationally based health ministries have been Christian churches. This is based in part on sheer numbers, in part on the historic role healing has played in Christianity, and in part on how the movement began. The language of health ministry has been distinctly Christian. While a great deal can be learned from studying health and healing in different religious traditions, I would suggest that culturally appropriate language needs to be found as health ministries grow in other religious traditions to uniquely express how health may fit into the life of synagogues, temples, and mosques.

The examples in this book are drawn from churches. I would invite readers from religious backgrounds other than Christianity to read thoughtfully, listening to what sounds consistent and inconsistent with your religious beliefs, and consider what words, symbols, and actions integrating faith and health would be meaningful in your particular religious context. For those working with congregations from traditions other than Christianity, the book's organizing framework of understanding congregational culture will be relevant to any religious tradition. The religious context of the tradition needs to be understood in order to learn how health might fit into the life of the local congregation.

MOTIVATIONS FOR HEALTH MINISTRY

What would motivate individuals and organizations to engage congregations in ministries of health? Health professionals may be interested in integrating faith into their professional practice in a congregational setting, including a growing number of parish nurses and health ministers. City and county departments of health may be interested in congregations as valued partners in addressing community health issues of mutual concern. Hospitals may be interested in engaging congregations through community outreach. Clergy may be interested in reclaiming the historic role of the church in health and healing as they respond to congregational and community concerns. Lay leaders in congregations may be interested in health and healing ministries to enliven the church.

Congregations will vary in their motivations for engaging in ministries of health. Some will find motivation in continuing a religious tradition of healing. Other congregations will be motivated by a desire for justice in matters of health, relieving suffering, or personal stewardship. A congregation must have a meaningful motivation to consider health as a ministry. Depending on how the congregation has understood their ministry, a motivation for why they should be involved in health ministries may be easily identified, or they may need assistance to see how this might be consistent with values they hold for ministry in general. A multidisciplinary perspective on health that considers biblical, theological, and denominational views on health as well as perspectives from the health fields can provide an understanding for the cultural context of health ministries and the potential for congregations to improve the health of their communities.

The growing interest in the actual and potential role of congregations to promote health, often manifested in the church through health ministries, and within the public health community through faith and health partnerships, is the result of a convergence of multiple factors. A knowledge base has been created that documents the influence of individual behavior on health as well as the positive influence of religious participation.[1] Society has recognized the limitations of our medical system to heal, and political realities have created issues in access to health care. An openness has emerged to discuss the interrelationships between faith and health, not only in congregations but in hospitals, departments of health, and medical research. In addition there is interest in complementary approaches to promoting health as we are increasingly faced with the limitations of our traditional medical care system. From the perspective of congregations, there is a new openness to considering health ministry as a way to revitalize and enhance the ministries of the church.

CONGREGATIONAL CULTURE AND HEALTH MINISTRIES

Health professionals and clergy working in health ministries need to be cognizant of both the dynamics of congregational culture and the dynamics of community health in order to optimize the ability of churches to promote the health of their congregation and their community. It is my belief, and the thesis of this book, that an understanding of congregational culture and a concern for the health of communities as well as individuals is essential. If health ministries are to fully develop their potential to positively influence the health of individuals, families, and communities, they need to develop in a manner consistent with the culture of the congregations in which they are housed. How any given congregation will understand and implement a health ministry will depend on their values, beliefs, and norms of behavior as well as their understanding of health. Consequently, health professionals and clergy working to engage congregations in promoting health need to be cognizant of the culture of congregations to ensure that as ministries develop they are congruent with the culture of the congregation, and thus sustainable over time.

Health ministry involves not only the culture of the congregation, but the culture of health care as well. It is intrinsically cross-cultural as these two cultures intertwine, with each bringing their own unique perspective on the interrelationships between faith and health. Health ministry is a cross-cultural experience because health brings with it all of the cultural values of the health care system and the individual health professions involved, and ministry brings with it all of the cultural values of professional ministry, the congregation, and wider ecclesiastical bodies. These are two very different cultures with different patterns of organization and language. Through collaboration, the culture of health care and the culture of ministry have the potential to transform the experience of health in ways that neither could accomplish alone.

COMMUNICATING HEALTH MINISTRY[2]

The language of health ministry is a significant reflection of its cross-cultural and interdisciplinary characteristics. As a compound term, health ministry joins health and ministry, including elements of both core concepts. Given its dual nature, health ministry should be meaningful to both health professionals and ministry professionals. Language that integrates health and ministry is needed to discuss the possibilities for health and healing within congregations.

Our ability to communicate is both enabled and limited by language.[3] This fundamental principle of anthropology is an important reminder for health ministry practice. When a term is compound, one word has to be first. Just as when we walk one foot has to lead, when a compound term is created a conscious decision has been made about which of the two concepts being joined will lead. In the case of health ministry, the lead term is health. This is not a coincidence. It reflects a particular worldview that comes from the culture of health professionals, the majority being nurses, attracted to the possibilities of promoting health in a church setting. So health leads with ministry following. Parish nursing is also a compound term and in that case parish, as the setting of care, leads. This is typical for nursing language where the adjective describes the area in which nursing care is provided, such as community health nursing, school nursing, or critical care nursing. Parish nursing has been attractive to nurses because nursing practice within a congregational setting provides the opportunity to further connect health and ministry, which may have been part of an initial impetus to pursue nursing as a vocation.[4]

There is nothing bad about having to choose the lead term when a new compound term is created; it is an inevitable limitation of our language, yet it is not without value. In choosing the lead term a value judgment is being made that says this term belongs first. So it has been with health ministries. Health defines the ministry. I suggest that the time has come to also talk about ministries of health. I believe the term "ministries of health" communicates something different than the term health ministry that may expand how congregations understand their role in promoting health.

When we work in a cross-cultural setting we need to find language that adequately communicates what is happening for everyone involved. As a nurse on the faculty of a seminary, I work daily in a professionally cross-cultural environment. In doing so, and through participating in the education of both pastors and health professionals, I have come to understand in a new way how our language both enables and limits our ability to communicate in the area of ministry and health. We cannot discuss concepts for which we have no words, or for which we have no words that others can easily understand. Reflecting on my experience with health ministry, I believe that while health professionals have been drawn to support this powerful idea, the future support of health ministries is dependent on churches understanding how faith and health are interrelated and why it is imperative to address issues of health within a congregation. I would suggest that a simple change in language, reflecting this understanding, would contribute to that process.

Over the past few years, I have found my language gradually changing from talking about health ministries to also include talking about ministries of health. Reflecting on this unintentional change, I found good reason for it. Health ministries happen within the context of a church. The church is the base of operations with theology providing the conceptual underpinnings. It is the church that will need to provide long-term support for health ministry. The health care environment will run hot and cold, with hospital-sponsored health ministry programs even in church-sponsored institutions continually vulnerable to budget cuts. However, the church will find ways to provide support when health is understood as essential to their mission.

Churches have a history of providing support for valued programs, and ministries rather than health provide the organizational framework.

I have found that not all congregations embrace the church's role in health whole heartedly. I would suggest that a revision in language might help clergy and church members better understand how health and healing fit into the life of a congregation. Talking about ministries of health rather than health ministries says that we first and foremost understand this as a ministry. Using the term health ministry can imply that health is being brought to the church where it will be a ministry. This is a very subtle difference, but one that I believe can make a difference.

You will note that I use the plural ministries rather than ministry, reflecting the multiple ministries of a church that can promote health. When we approach ministries of health from the perspective of how they fit into the culture and understanding of the congregation rather than how we can bring health services to the church, or how health professionals can use their expertise in the church setting, we will make major inroads into ensuring the future of the church's role in health and healing.

Realistically, there are times when health ministry is the preferred grammatical form, and I am not suggesting that all the existing uses of health ministry, including those in my job title, be abandoned. In fact, you will note that I use both terms throughout this book for our consideration. However, I would suggest that the thinking reflected behind this conceptual change could gradually have a positive influence on our congregations. To that end, I offer my definition of ministries of health:

> Ministries of health are the components of church life that promote the health, healing, and wholeness of individuals, families, congregations, and communities. Ministries of health may have an explicit purpose to promote health or they may have a purpose other than health promotion, yet health, healing, and wholeness are enhanced through participation in that ministry.

Ministries of health, then, is the broader term, with health ministries referring to those activities in which a church intentionally engages for the explicit purpose of promoting health.

COMMUNITY AND HEALTH MINISTRIES

The importance of community health to congregationally based health ministries forms the second premise of this book. While much has been done, and can be done, to positively influence the health of individuals through health ministries, the full potential of integrating faith and health will be missed if the focus is only on individuals, families, and congregations. The time is ripe to use the inherent strengths of congregations and build on their core values to improve the health of communities as well. Churches are well represented in any community and integral to neighborhood life. The gospel they preach has a message of restoring wholeness through faith, compatible with the public health message of promoting community health based on humanitarian interests. While congregations and departments of health have different motivations, they share a mutual interest in improving community well-being.[5]

Interdisciplinary collaboration is integral to community health. One of the unique characteristics of health ministry is the collaboration between congregations and health care organizations, and between health professionals and clergy. Health ministry requires a variety of health professionals, clergy, and interested lay people in order to reach its full potential. Therefore any understanding of health ministry needs to involve dialogue between disciplines and between institutions.

Health professionals have much to learn from ministry professionals about the theology of health and biblical perspectives on health and healing. Ministry professionals have much to learn from health professionals about the influence of lifestyle on health. Many disciplines are contributing to the growth in health ministries. In health care, nursing has been on the forefront of health ministries through parish nursing. Medical research has delved into the interrelationships between religion and health. Public health has provided an emphasis on community health as it has identified congregations as effective partners in addressing community health issues. Health professionals from many disciplines have been involved in medical missions in Third World countries, integrating faith and health in very practical ways. Biblical scholars inform us of the rich images of health and healing found in the Bible. Theologians challenge us regarding what it means to be embodied. Pastoral care reminds us of the spiritual issues raised in times of illness. Practical theology provides an understanding of why health is an appropriate concern of the church. Ethicists challenge us with the religious and personal significance of health care decisions.

Other fields contribute to the interdisciplinary work of health ministries as well. Assets-based community development highlights the importance of congregations working with community strengths rather than focusing on community needs to address health issues of mutual concern. Politics has opened new possibilities for partnerships between the government and faith-based organizations, demonstrated by the creation of the White House Office on Faith-Based and Community Initiatives in 2001. Philanthropy has contributed to the development of health ministries as foundations have provided support to develop health ministries, recognizing the creative potential for churches to address community health problems.

There are many ways that congregations have a positive influence on health without ever intentionally trying to promote health. In medical research this has been demonstrated through looking at the association between religious practices and personal health, and has also been supported in my own research. When the church is fulfilling its purpose it will provide meaning, worship experiences, opportunities for service, a sense of connectedness, and social support, all of which can have a positive impact on health. This can be considered the intrinsic health ministry of the church.[6]

In addition, congregations have the potential to do more to improve health through the cross-cultural and interdisciplinary work of health ministries. An increasing number of congregations are choosing to reclaim the historic role of the church in health and healing through developing intentional ministries of health that address health issues of concern to individuals, families, and communities. The relevance of health to the life of the church is indisputable. Many issues requiring pastoral care have a health component, such as illness, disability, birth, parenting, aging, divorce, substance abuse, and death. The significance of health to worship life is further reflected in the tradition of healing services.[7]

FOUNDATIONS FOR MINISTRIES OF HEALTH

Understanding the meaning of health, healing, and wholeness within the context of a particular congregation is foundational to ministries of health, as discussed in chapter 2. How both health and ministry are understood by the congregation will influence the approach to health ministry. What religious teachings of the congregation contribute to an understanding of health that can be used to develop ministries? What are the connecting points between sacred texts and an understanding of health? For example, a congregation concerned about the biblical emphasis on justice may be interested in a local, regional, national, or global approach that deals with issues of access to health care. A congregation with an emphasis on a personal faith experience may find the interrelationships between body/mind/spirit for individuals an appealing motivation. Knowing the sacred texts that inform the life of the congregation and understanding the views held within the congregation on the meaning of health and the meaning of ministry will be invaluable in identifying the motivational factors unique to a particular congregation that would inspire ministries of health.

Understanding the historic context of health ministries is valuable when seeking to engage congregations in ministries of health. Chapter 3 explores the reasons why the faith and health movement in general, and congregationally based health ministries in particular, have emerged at this time in our society.

Multiple intersecting dynamics have converged to make health ministries particularly relevant in today's congregations. The key contributing factors include reclaiming historic traditions, social trends, developments in health care, a changing paradigm of health, trends in religion, and growth in faith and health organizations. Each individual congregation will be affected by this contemporary social context as well as their own unique history and tradition.

To understand the specifics of any given congregation as it relates to health ministries, we build on the work of congregational studies in creating a body of knowledge for understanding the values, beliefs, and cultures of congregations of any religious belief. The significance of understanding congregational culture as a tool for engaging congregations in ministries of health is interwoven throughout this book and the focus of chapter 4. Understanding the cultural dynamics of the particular congregation will increase the likelihood that ministries developed will be congruent with the values and beliefs of the congregation.

Working with congregational and community strengths to develop health ministries is part of understanding congregation culture. Assets-based community development gives insight into the importance of working with strengths and resources rather than focusing on problems and needs. Chapter 5 examines this valuable approach and considers the unique strengths shared by congregations in general. Strategies are identified for discovering the particular strengths and resources of any given congregation in order to create meaningful and relevant health ministries for both the congregation and the community.

Health ministries that build on the assets of the congregation and the community can have a positive influence not only on individuals, but on families and communities as well. Individuals experience health and illness within their own bodies. Yet, the community both provides and limits opportunities for health as well as defines the meaning of health and illness. The opportunities for health and the meaning of health cannot be separated from the environment in which we live and the persons with whom we share this environment. Churches are in a unique position to foster the communal dimensions of health because community is an essential part of congregational life. Chapter 6 examines this unique potential to promote community health.

We move from exploring the church's potential to promote community health to discovering the possibilities for faith and health partnerships in chapter 7. Congregations seeking to work with their communities in ministries of health will find that a model of partnership and identifying community strengths rather than focusing on problems will be empowering to both the congregation and the community. All communities have strengths and resources that can be brought to bear on issues of mutual concern in health ministries, whatever their economic status. In partnerships, the cultures of all organizations involved need to be considered in order to create an appropriate relationship consistent with the values and beliefs of all partners. Around the nation, faith and health partnerships have been created to deal with a wide range of issues including early detection of cancer, HIV/AIDS, and violence prevention.

Whether working in a partnership or independently, congregations will find there are many different models for health ministry from which to choose, including a health cabinet, parish nursing, health ministers, lay health promoters, faith-based clinics, caring congregations, or ministries focused on a specific health-related issue, as discussed in chapter 8. Whatever model of health ministry a congregation chooses, it is important that it be consistent with the values and beliefs of the congregation. The appropriate model of health ministry for a particular congregation will be determined by the congregation's vision, what they are trying to accomplish, and the available human resources, finances, and support.

No consideration of engaging congregations in ministries of health would be complete without considering the infrastructure needed to make health ministries sustainable. I address this overarching concern in chapter 9. In addition to organizational and financial resources needed for continuation, integrating health ministry into the fabric of the congregation must be considered so health ministry does not become just another well-intentioned program. A culturally congruent health ministry must have a congregational infrastructure for ongoing support if it is to be more than the passion of one individual or group at a particular point in time. Partnering organizations need to be mindful of developing continuing support as well. If an initiative is related to grant funding, how will the congregation be able to continue the work when funding ends and/or the partnership is no longer active?

In order to ensure continued support for health ministries, issues of accountability need to be addressed and methods for evaluating the effectiveness of the health ministry in place. Typically congregations are very informal in their evaluation methods. Yet for congregations in partnership with health care organizations or receiving external funding, evaluation methods are expected as an essential component of continued support. The long-term future of health ministries will be dependent on how churches assess the significance of health ministry to their communal life, and how partnering organizations evaluate the ability of health ministry to meet their desired outcomes.

VISION FOR HEALTH MINISTRY

I present a vision for health ministry in the final chapter, as I consider the future for this emerging field. Congregations will have made important strides in realizing their potential to promote health when they look beyond their doors to the communities in which they live. Consistent with our Western mindset on individualism, it is often easier to focus on issues of individual health. This is important because much can be done to have a positive influence on the health of individuals. However, I believe that congregations will have their greatest impact through ministries of health when they take on the challenge to be communities of healing. Congregations become healing communities when they bring people in, when they include outsiders and listen to their story. Congregations also become healing communities when they engage in acts of compassion, mercy, and justice that create physical, psychosocial, spiritual, economic environments where health for all is possible. Building on a biblical foundation, congregations have the power to transform the health of individuals, families, and communities as they continue Christ's healing ministry.

QUESTIONS FOR REFLECTION

1. What and/or who is driving interest in health ministry, at this time, for this congregation?

2. How open is this congregation to the idea of health ministries?

3. Is there any reason why this would not be a good time to explore health ministries?

4. What additional information is needed before beginning to engage in ministries of health?

IDEAS FOR CONGREGATIONAL ENGAGEMENT

1. Talk with people from nearby congregations or from other churches from the same denomination involved in health ministries to find out about their experience.

2. Hold an exploratory meeting with interested persons in the congregation.

2

HEALTH, HEALING, AND WHOLENESS

A Health Ministry Perspective

L ong before there was a faith and health movement I learned about health, healing, and wholeness at the side of my father, who was a minister in a small New England town. As a young child I would go with him on house calls or hospital visits. We would visit people in their homes, on their farms, and in the hospital. I remember this time with my father fondly and think of it as my first exposure to the connections between faith and health. I learned this connection at his side without it ever being explicitly expressed. I learned that matters of health were an important part of ministry. In the rhythm of life in the country, I learned about wholeness and what it means to be part of a caring community.

For each of us, the pursuit of health is both a personal and a communal quest shaped by multiple perspectives on the meaning of health. These different understandings of health need to be understood when engaging a congregation in ministries of health. Reflecting on what health means for you personally and learning what it means for members of the congregation provide a critical foundation. Learning more about biblical and theological viewpoints on health, as well as perspectives of the health professions, is crucial to the interdisciplinary work at hand. To this end, health professionals will find they need to learn more about biblical and theological perspectives on health. Clergy will find they need to learn more about the dynamics of health. "Faith needs the language of health in order to understand how it applies to life; health needs the language of faith in order to find its larger context, its meaning."[1] It is this rich collaborative work that makes health ministry meaningful.

COMMUNITY AND HEALTH IN THE BIBLE

When churches today consider how they might engage in ministries of health, they can begin looking to the Bible for guidance. While congregations vary in their use of scripture, the Bible informs the life of all Christian churches. For individuals, understanding biblical texts relevant to health can illuminate the interrelationship between faith and health. For health ministry leaders and clergy, being conversant with key biblical concepts related to health is central to making the case for why and how health may be a ministry. For congregations, exploring biblical concepts of health may provide the inspiration and vision to create new ministries.

Two biblical themes are of particular significance for health ministries: the role of the community in health, and the concept of wholeness.[2] Individualism and dualism are not found in the Bible, which focuses on the health of the community rather than individual health. Wholeness of being that defies separation into physical, mental, or spiritual components expresses health in scripture.[3]

The Old Testament makes a strong case for the role and responsibility of the community to ensure health for all. While there are many individuals of significance, God deals primarily with Israel as a community. Their importance is as a people in relationship with God with an emphasis on life in community. Righteousness and having a right relationship with God are significant to health in the Old Testament. God is righteous and calls the people of Israel to be in right relationship with God, themselves, their fellow human beings, and their environment. Being in right relationship contributes to well-being.[4] In Exodus 15:26 God affirms the relational nature of health. "If you will listen carefully to the voice of the LORD your God, and do what is right in his sight, and give heed to his commandments and keep all his statutes, I will not bring upon you any of the diseases that I brought upon the Egyptians; for I am the LORD who heals you." While certainly there is intent for individuals to have a right relationship with God and assume personal responsibility, it is the community's relationship with God that is of greatest significance.

Justice is another Old Testament theme relevant to community and health, both in biblical times and today.[5] God is continually calling upon the people of Israel to act in a just way that will restore the wholeness God intends for the world. God is calling Israel to be in right relationship with God and act in a just manner, which will restore healing and wholeness to all God's people.

> Is this not the fast that I choose: to loose the bonds of injustice, to undo the thongs of the yoke, to let the oppressed go free, and to break every yoke? Is it not to share your bread with the hungry, and bring the homeless poor into your house; when you see the naked, to cover them, and not to hide yourself from your own kin? Then your light shall break forth like the dawn, and your healing shall spring up quickly . . .
>
> *–Isaiah 58:6–8a*

In the New Testament one cannot read far without noticing how important healing was in Jesus' ministry. While Jesus healed people individually, the role of community is ever present in the background. Illness is experienced by individuals, but within the context of their community that shapes the meaning of the experience. Illness in biblical times, and today as well, removes individuals from full participation in their communities. Jesus' acts of healing restored individuals to their communal life. The significance of the illnesses Jesus healed was not found in their physical characteristics. Rather, the significance of healing in biblical times was the meaning it held for the individual and the community.[6] Restoring health was so important that it is part of the mandate Jesus gave his disciples when they were called together and given power and authority over all demons and to cure diseases, and sent out to proclaim the reign of God and to heal (Luke 9:1–2).

HEALING AND WHOLENESS

Healing restores wholeness to individuals and to communities. Our relationship with self and others is illuminated in the biblical images of wholeness significant to contemporary health ministries. The Hebrew language does not have the concept of body, mind, and spirit as separate entities. It consistently presents a more holistic understanding of reality than we find in Western languages. Humans are a living *nephesh*, understood as a unity of body and soul. Because the English language doesn't have the same concept, *nephesh* is sometimes translated incompletely as "I" or "me," sometimes as "soul."[7] This essential understanding of personal wholeness that contrasts with dualistic Western thinking is being reclaimed in the faith and health movement today.

The Hebrew term *shalom* is considered the concept most closely related to the term health in the Bible. Shalom is often translated as "peace," but it means much more than that. It incorporates peace, prosperity, rest, safety, security, justice, happiness, health, welfare, and wholeness. In the Old Testament shalom is used when there is harmony between people and between people and things.[8] To be in harmony means to live in peace with someone or something. To be in good health, a person must live in harmony.

The Old Testament concept of shalom is connected to the New Testament concept of salvation. Salvation can be understood as healing with cosmic significance. The purpose of Jesus' coming was to provide salvation that would restore the wholeness of shalom God intended for creation. This is the ultimate experience of health for the Christian. The story of scripture is the story of God's efforts to restore wholeness.[9] Health, healing, and salvation, while experienced by individuals, are essentially communal experiences, and the health of individuals is in part dependent on the health of the community.[10]

Healing is the restoration of health. We can learn about health indirectly by looking at what it is that healing restores. Consider the restoration of wholeness. Many Christian traditions understand wholeness of body/mind/spirit as God's will for all of creation. Wholeness is pursued through mending the brokenness caused by sin that separates humans from God. To be whole is to be in relationship with God and others. Healing that seeks to restore wholeness involves restoring these relationships. This search for wholeness is a lifelong spiritual journey that becomes complete only after death when God is seen face to face.[11] From this perspective, health reflected in wholeness is understood as a process rather than a state to be achieved. There is always a need for healing because of the inherently broken nature of humankind.

UNDERSTANDINGS OF HEALTH

The community's role in health and an understanding of wholeness have also been articulated by denominations, theologians, and health professionals as they have explored the multifaceted nature of health. Health ministers need to be bilingual—able to converse in both matters of health and matters of theology related to health. Of course one will have a "native" language, but some familiarity with both languages is needed.

Articulating a definition of health is important because how health is understood will influence how health promotion is understood and how health ministries are envisioned. There is a common tendency when defining health to make it synonymous with physical health. Yet there is more to health and well-being than the state of the body. Individuals know experientially that body/mind/spirit, while distinct words, are experienced as an interrelated whole. When health is understood from an integrated perspective that goes beyond physical well-being, the relationship between faith and health becomes increasingly evident.[12] Consider, for example, the consequence of defining health as the absence of disease. Health promotion is then likely to concentrate on disease prevention and health ministry is likely to focus on providing direct health services. If health is understood as harmony with self, others, the environment, and God, then addressing environmental issues and/or nurturing spiritual development may be a logical approach to health ministries.

Denominations have been involved in defining and understanding health as they have sought to continue Jesus' ministry of healing and to support local congregations in ministries of health. The very fact that denominations are articulating an understanding of health is one reflection of the relevance of health to the local church. While individual congregations may or may not be in agreement with their denominational statements, they reflect a particular theological perspective with practical implications for how a church might promote health. Table 1 includes several definitions of health from denominational materials on health ministries.

Table 1   UNDERSTANDING HEALTH: DENOMINATIONS

Evangelical Lutheran Church of America "Health is a gift. . . . Health is finite. . . . Health is neighborly. . . . Health is social responsibility. . . . Health is a matter of justice in society. . . . Health is more than a marketplace item."[13]

Presbyterian Church USA "Health is the ability to respond to a wide variety of challenges, living up to potential and promise. . . . For Christians, the definition of health goes beyond curing disease or traumas, beyond even a preventive and wellness model, to embrace a concept of wholeness. Jesus not only restored persons to physical health but, in the process, righted relationships with others in the community and with God. . . . Health and wholeness, however, are not dependent on the absence of impairment or on physical perfection. One can be injured, possessed of a disabling condition, malformed of body, and yet be 'healthy.'"[14]

United Church of Christ "Health is harmony with self, others, the environment and with God—a continuum of physical, social, psychological, and spiritual well-being."[15]

For theologians, understanding health is an issue of personal and religious significance. For practical theologians the challenge is to understand the significance of health to the life and ministry of the church. From a theological perspective an understanding of health always involves supporting the health of the community.[16] While health professionals providing health ministry leadership do not need to know all of the biblical and theological nuances regarding health, they do need to be familiar with how health has been addressed in biblical studies, in the work of denominations, and by theologians. Table 2 includes several theological perspectives on health.

Table 2 **UNDERSTANDING HEALTH: THEOLOGY/PASTORAL CARE**

James Wind "Hold on to the fleeting image of the seventh day because in it we see God's intent: humans and all other creatures at ease, in harmony, resting in the presence of the Creator. Our first picture of health, then, is an ecological one, a picture of people in perfect relation to God, neighbor, self, and cosmos."[17]

Leo Thomas and Jan Alkire Health is "a sharing in the wholeness of God. Bringing a person into this reality is the ultimate goal of the ministry of religious healing. Becoming sharers in the wholeness of God is a lifelong process, called the spiritual journey, that involves every dimension of our being. Our transformation will be complete when we see God face to face."[18]

James Evans "In African traditional and African Christian thought, health is understood as harmony and disease as disharmony."[19]

The health professions are the final group to which we look for meanings of health. Historically they have defined health as the absence of disease. However, definitions have changed as a broader understanding of the dynamics of health has evolved. Table 3 includes definitions from medicine, nursing, and public health that reflect a holistic community health perspective.

Table 3 **UNDERSTANDING HEALTH: HEALTH PROFESSIONS**

Christian Medical Commission, World Council of Churches
"Health is a dynamic state of well-being of the individual and
society; of physical, mental, spiritual, economic, political, and
social well-being; of being in harmony with each other, with
the material environment and with God. Well-being refers to
our dynamic contact with the Source of our Being, and as
Christians, we believe that it is Jesus Christ that gives us life."
In looking at health from an international perspective, the
commission goes on to say that health is an issue of justice, of
peace, of the integrity of creation as well as a spiritual issue.[20]

Afaf Meleis "Health is a personal commitment, but it is also a
social commitment. And it is a social commitment within a
group. . . . Health is to manage, health is to negotiate, health is
to achieve for a group, not to achieve for the self. . . . Health is
to grow within a group, and have the group or the family grow,
and health is to be part of that group. And health is to think
about the environment and look at it, look at the entire environment to understand the person."[21]

World Health Organization A commonly referenced definition of
health comes from the World Health Organization originally articulated in 1946. This was one of the earliest definitions of health
to include a holistic perspective. "Health is a dynamic state of
complete physical, mental, and social well-being and not merely
the absence of disease or infirmity."[22]

Socioeconomic factors influence both the experience and understanding of health. Health ministry leaders need to be
aware how socioeconomic status influences their own perception of health, and the perceptions of the persons with whom
they minister. A person who lives with social and economic
challenges is likely to have a very different perspective on
health and what contributes to well-being than someone in a
position of social and economic privilege. Considering health

as a social matter includes understanding health as relief from worry and fear of violence, and access to health care choices.[23]

Examining these different perspectives reveals the multi-faceted nature of health. Practically speaking, the question for health ministry leaders becomes how these definitions might be reflected in action and used to help engage a congregation in ministries of health.

THE CALL TO HEALTH MINISTRIES

Health ministry has been described to include any of the following: the work of a parish nurse or health minister with a congregation; an understanding that an extension of the work of Jesus Christ is to heal the sick and promote health and wholeness;[24] the community life of a congregation including worship, fellowship, education, and service that strives to promote wholeness; congregation-based education programs addressing health issues; advocacy and support programs for persons marginalized by disease or disability; and the provision of direct health services by a Christian group locally;[25] or globally through missionaries.[26]

The intentional health ministry of the church is multidimensional. Health ministry involves empowering individuals, families, and communities to achieve health and wholeness within the context of ministry. It can include wellness ministry that seeks to promote health. Health ministry may also include healing ministry that seeks to restore health and health care ministry providing direct care.

Whatever the approach, promoting health and enhancing well-being is an important part of health ministry. Consequently, it is imperative to consider what enables people to be well. A health professional considering this question might talk about health promotion activities and decreasing risky behaviors. Addressing the same question from a faith perspective, we might talk about life affirming attitudes and behaviors that enhance health and life denying attitudes and behaviors that diminish health. For churches engaged in ministries of health the question becomes how to nurture environments in congregations and communities where health for all is possible in the broadest sense.

DYNAMICS OF HEALTH MINISTRY

Health is a process, not a static state—it moves toward wholeness through health promotion, disease prevention, and coping with chronic conditions. Similarly, health ministry is a process rather than a program, although it will include programs. The programs, classes, or events in a health ministry are a means to an end, rather than an end in themselves. At its best, health ministry is a process of integrating health and healing into the faith life of the church in ways that are life affirming. Health ministry challenges the congregation to reflect on how its life in community promotes health, healing, and wholeness. To this end, health ministry may incorporate committees, but health ministry is not a committee. Health ministry has the potential to be integrated in all aspects of the church: in worship, education, outreach, and service. Health ministry is not the exclusive domain of health professionals or the health care system, although they will be invaluable resources for any health ministry. Everyone has something to contribute to health ministries. At its best, health involves the whole church.[27]

In addition to being understood as a process, health ministry can also be understood as an imperative, a program, or a consequence. Understanding health ministry as a process involves conceptualizing the meaning of health and how it can be achieved while working to integrate health throughout the life of the church. Understanding health ministry as an imperative finds the motivation for health ministry in biblical concepts such as justice, loving one's neighbor, and the healing ministry of Jesus, making us reach out to others within and beyond the church. Understanding health ministry as program leads to actualizing health ministry through specific activities, of which there are many to choose. Understanding health ministry as consequence recognizes and affirms the inherently health promoting qualities of congregational life, and builds on the intrinsic health ministry of the church to intentionally promote health.

Congregations need a reason to fully engage in ministries of health. Some may easily identify a reason; some may require assistance to understand how health promotion is consistent with their values for ministry. The congregation will need to answer, "Why should we be involved in health ministries? How does it fit with our mission, vision, values, and purpose as we understand them?" Religious motivations such as continuing the tradition of Jesus' healing ministry, addressing issues of injustice, relieving suffering, and personal stewardship of one's body may inspire a church, as may practical or political motivations. Providing church members an opportunity to explore new areas of ministry or connecting to the right people or organizations at the right time may be as important as any biblical or theological concepts that support health ministries. In either case, understanding the culture of the congregation will illuminate ways to discuss health, healing, and wholeness in ways that engage this particular group.

As we consider health, healing, and wholeness in meaningful ways for the church's ministries of health, remember the community's importance in promoting health. Essayist Wendell Berry wrote "community—in the fullest sense: a place and all its creatures—is the smallest unit of health . . ."[28] The wholeness of individuals requires experiencing the wholeness of being part of meaningful community.[29] Even when ministering with individuals, congregations need to recognize that persons experience their health and illness in the context of a community that can either facilitate or limit the opportunities for health. Today's churches need to reach beyond their doors to their neighborhoods to positively influence community health. The challenges and opportunities of contemporary society provide a unique opportunity to name and reclaim the church's history in health and healing as we pursue health, healing, and wholeness for all.

QUESTIONS FOR REFLECTION

1. Write your own personal definition of health. What and who shapes your personal understanding of health?

2. How can a biblical understanding of the role of community in promoting health be applied to the congregation(s) with which you are working?

3. What are your reflections or critique on the definitions of health listed in Tables 1–3? Have any of these definitions presented a dimension of health you had not thought about previously?

4. What motivations for engaging in ministries of health might be meaningful to the congregation(s) with which you are working?

IDEAS FOR CONGREGATIONAL ENGAGEMENT

1. Organize a Bible study of Isaiah 58:5–12. Consider the following questions:

   – What does this passage tell us about what is required to be healthy?
   – Where does the responsibility for health lie, with the individual or with the community?
   – What is the relationship between individual and community health?
   – How might this congregation respond to the challenge for health and healing presented in this passage?

2. Organize a Bible study of Jesus' ministry of healing, such as in Mark 5:25–34 or Luke 17:11–19. Consider the following questions:

   – Who initiates the healing in this story?
   – What causes the healing?
   – What does this story of healing tell us about health?
   – What lessons can we learn from this passage that might be used in our ministries of health?

3. Organize a discussion about "What does God have to do with health?" Invite health professionals and clergy to participate.

4. Talk with people in the church individually or in a focus group about what being healthy means to them, what they do to keep healthy, and how, if at all, they experience a relationship between their faith and health.

3

THE CONTEMPORARY CONTEXT
FOR HEALTH MINISTRIES

The growing interest in churches promoting health is the result of multiple cultural factors converging. Grounded in the historic roots of the church, affected by trends in society, influenced by contemporary developments in health care, informed by a transforming paradigm of health, shaped by changes in the religious environment, and supported by emerging faith and health organizations, the faith and health ministries movement is the product of a unique time in American history. While the idea of religious organizations being involved in health and healing goes back to biblical times, the use of the term health ministry is a recent phenomenon. Long before there were hospitals or departments of health, Christians were caring for the health and well-being of others. When the modern concept of health ministries emerged in the 1980s it was not a new idea but rather the reclamation of an ancient idea.

My current position as a nurse on the faculty of a theological seminary teaching interdisciplinary classes in faith and health is one reflection of the contemporary dynamics contributing to the current interest in health ministries. Ten years ago there were no such classes and few churches in our denomination with health ministries. Now there is growing interest among health professionals, clergy, and seminarians in our faith and health classes and a growing number of churches with health ministries. All of our Master of Divinity students are now required to take a spiritual formation class on embodiment. What had not been imagined ten years ago has now become essential. Truly this is a unique time in history for the integration of faith and health.

As we consider six contemporary dynamics contributing to the current interest in health ministries (Figure 1), be mindful of any additional local and regional factors that may be operative in your community.

Figure 1: Contemporary Dynamics of Health Ministries

Reclaiming Historic Traditions

Growth of Faith and Health Organizations

Trends in Society

HEALTH MINISTRIES

Trends in Religion

Developments in Health Care

Changing Health Paradigm

RECLAIMING HISTORIC TRADITIONS

The current context for health ministries is rooted in the history of the church. History is not just about what happened in the past, it also enlightens the present. The process of introducing health ministries to a congregation is informed by an understanding of how the church has fluctuated between embracing and ignoring its role in restoring health over time. One way of encouraging the church to reclaim this birthright and create new ministries of health is to name this historic tradition and to identify traces of its roots in the contemporary church.

While early Christians enthusiastically embraced healing as they continued Jesus' ministry, the role of healing in the church eroded over time as beliefs and practices changed and medicine emerged as a profession. Eventually caring for sick or dying persons rather than cure became the emphasis of the church's healing ministry. This was manifested in the late nineteenth and early twentieth century by the creation of church affiliated hospitals, nursing homes, orphanages, and hospices. There has been a gradual decline over the past century in religiously sponsored hospitals, and the responsibility to care for the sick has been largely turned over to the medical profession.[1]

The growth of medical missions has also been significant in the church's history in health care. Medical missions were seen as a response to the needs of people around the world as well as an opportunity to spread the gospel. Contemporary health ministries have been influenced by this work in missions as the importance of working with the local culture to develop culturally congruent health initiatives has been recognized. Dr. James Alley, a former medical missionary, appointed state health officer for Georgia in 1978, was one of the first to develop partnerships between churches and public health, working particularly with local churches in the African American community.[2] One of the early pieces articulating a holistic and global view of health ministries, *Healing and Wholeness: The Churches' Role in Health,* produced by the Christian Medical Commission of the World Council of Churches, was also influenced by a medical mission perspective.[3]

Two additional traditions have created historic patterns contributing to the contemporary relevance of health ministries. The deaconess role of women trained to care for the poor and the sick has been utilized periodically since biblical times. The social gospel movement of the late nineteenth century found the deaconess a fitting role for its ministries, and many deaconesses provided care in the community and in newly formed hospitals. This tradition, which continues to be used in Scandinavia, is considered by some to be a precursor to today's parish nurses.[4]

The role of the church nurse or nursing board in many African American congregations is another historic tradition contributing to today's health ministries. For many years nursing boards have provided first aid and care to members during worship services. The church nurse is not necessarily a licensed nurse, but a person who is seen as capable, caring, and compassionate. The existence of such a role represents an identified health need within church life.[5] In my own experience working with African American churches with nursing boards, it was often this group that provided leadership for an expanded health ministry role.

The wholistic health movement in the 1970s laid important ground work for today's ministries of health. Led by Rev. Granger Westberg, a visionary Lutheran chaplain, this movement created a framework of caring for people as bio-psychosocial-spiritual beings.[6] Rev. Westberg was a leader in articulating the interrelationships between body, mind, and spirit. He worked with the University of Illinois and the Kellogg Foundation to develop wholistic health centers providing primary health care in church settings with interdisciplinary teams of physicians, nurses, and pastoral care counselors. The word wholistic was used instead of the traditional term holistic to better represent the concept of wholeness. The wholistic health movement not only created new models of health ministry, but also began to create an integrated language for the faith and health movement.

While conceptually productive, the wholistic health center proved to be cost-ineffective. However, from this experience came Rev. Westberg's idea of parish nursing: nurses working with congregations to promote health and provide a bridge between the health care system and the community of faith. The first parish nurse programs were created in the mid 1980s in the Midwest.[7] While parish nursing is only one of several health ministry models, the interest in parish nursing has contributed to developing the broader concept of congregations as places of health and healing.

Concurrent to the development of wholistic health centers and the beginning of parish nursing, another approach to health ministries was emerging in the southeastern United States. Long before the term health ministry became popular, public health professionals were working with churches to train lay health advisors to provide basic health education and advocacy. Also known as lay health promoters or community health workers, this approach proved particularly effective in communities where issues of income, language, or culture make the community health worker a more accessible venue for receiving health information.[8]

TRENDS IN SOCIETY

Significant recent events in reclaiming the church's historic tradition in health have been affected by concurrent social trends. There is a growing interest in secular spirituality and health not associated with a particular religion, evidenced by the popularity of the work of physician authors such as Larry Dossey.[9] Growing interest in complementary medicine taps into both spirituality and dissatisfaction with the health care system, as evidenced in the growth of holistic health centers providing complementary therapies.[10]

The philanthropic community has reflected another social trend. Grant funding has helped begin or expand many health ministry programs. In addition, as nonprofit hospitals have been sold, the assets have been put into conversion foundations, which frequently continue a mission of promoting health in the community. Many of these foundations, such as Queens Care in Los Angeles County, California, and the Deaconess Foundation in St. Louis, Missouri, began with the sale of religiously affiliated hospitals and have continued the mission of faith-based health care through funding on the congregational level.

Changes in government structures and practices have created new possibilities for collaboration. The creation of the White House Office on Faith-Based and Community Initiatives in 2001 reflected an official national awareness of the tremendous role faith-based organizations play in supporting community well-being. Federal departments such as the Health Resource Service Administration have added their own initiatives with faith-based organizations, and local health departments now frequently work with congregations.

DEVELOPMENTS IN HEALTH CARE

Health care financing changes have contributed to the evolution of health ministry, as the growing influence of government on health care funding and the rise of for-profit health care institutions has displaced some of the need for religiously sponsored health care. Yet the Christian church's mandate for continuing the healing ministry of Jesus persists, so churches and denominations have struggled with how to have a relevant ministry of health today.[11] The current inability of the health care system to adequately finance health care access is a justice issue of concern to many faith traditions. Many religious groups worked collaboratively to support universal health care during the 1980s through the National Interfaith Health Care Campaign. More recently, the Faith Project of the Universal Health Care Action Network has engaged congregations in working for affordable accessible health care for all.[12]

In addition, the provision of health care has increasingly moved from hospitals to communities, of which congregations are an integral part, while simultaneously the increase in medical technology has made hospital-based health care more complex, more costly, and less personal. Changes in the public health system as well have created a climate ripe for faith and health partnerships. As funding for public health has diminished, creative approaches to addressing community health problems have included working with churches to provide health education, screening, and direct services. Following the example of the United States, other countries such as Canada[13] and Australia[14] have responded to a changing health care environment by developing parish nursing or faith community nursing.

Within the health care system, trends in nursing, public health, and medicine have had a significant influence on the evolution of health ministry. Nursing has been at the forefront of health ministry development. Nurses work as parish nurses and health ministry coordinators, and they supervise lay health promoters, and provide health ministry education. The ability of the nursing profession to provide a bridge between medicine and the public has lent itself well to these new roles in the community.

On the institutional side, a decline in the average length of patient stay in hospitals fueled by economic constraints and changing staffing patterns has altered the nursing work environment, changing the pace for both nurse and patient. Many nurses find the opportunity to provide nursing care in a relaxed setting conducive to long-term relationships a reason to consider parish nursing. An increasing number of nurses are working in community settings, including nurses serving congregations either in paid or unpaid roles as parish nurses or health ministers. The growing number of nurses and other health professionals willing to volunteer their services in health ministry reflects both an interest and a desire for a different kind of professional experience increasingly hard to find in traditional health care.[15]

Public health professionals have identified the church as a prime site for health interventions to reach underserved populations due to the strength of the congregation as a community organization, as well as a growing recognition of the interconnectedness between faith and health.[16] Partnering with churches, synagogues, and mosques has become an acceptable, and expected, way to address community health problems.

Physicians are acknowledging that health is more than the absence of disease and medicine has taken a new interest in the influence of spirituality and religious behavior on health. Dr. Herbert Benson of the Harvard/Mind/Body Institute, who wrote about the relaxation response in his book *Timeless Healing*, was one of the first physicians to do research on spirituality and health. The Institute's national professional conferences on religion, spirituality, and health have contributed to interdisciplinary dialogue on this topic. Harold Koenig of the Center for the Study of Religion/Spirituality and Health at Duke University has been a prolific physician author on the relationships between religion, spirituality, and health. The literature from these doctors and others has been disseminated in the popular as well as the professional press and contributes to the public discourse on matters of religion, spirituality, and health. The federal government's response to this growing interest was to establish the National Center for Complementary and Alternative Medicine in 1998 to support research, training, and education.

CHANGING HEALTH PARADIGM

Our knowledge of what it means to be healthy has changed radically, as has our understanding of what keeps people well. At the same time public health knowledge continues to demonstrate the impact of community based interventions on the health status of individuals. We have moved from a time when understanding health as the absence of disease made sense because the major causes of death were infectious diseases, to a time when the major causes of death are chronic illnesses that are greatly impacted by individual lifestyle and environmental and sociopolitical factors.[17] The influence of individual behavior on health and the potential influence of religious beliefs on behavior are seen as one rationale for health ministry. While the church has a long history in matters of healing, it has not had a strong history of health promotion.[18] New territory is being charted.

TRENDS IN RELIGION

Trends in religion have helped shape the current interest in health ministries, as churches have participated in the evolution of this concept both independently and through denominations. Medical missionaries both within and outside the United States have been one traditional way churches fulfilled their mandate to heal. With the changing health care environment and a changing missionary environment denominations have looked for other ways to fulfill their mandate to heal. Missionary work has provided important insight for health ministry in the United States by demonstrating the importance of community development in health promotion.[19]

Concurrent to changes in the mission field, many mainline Protestant churches have experienced a steady decline in membership and denominationalism. This has led to an interest in new approaches for staying relevant in contemporary society,[20] of which health ministries are one example. Churches are now reclaiming the tradition of health and healing and giving it new expression in congregationally based health ministries. Denominations have responded to the growing interest in health ministries with the creation of educational materials, task forces, health ministry networks, and resource staff.[21]

GROWTH OF FAITH AND HEALTH ORGANIZATIONS

Changes in the health professions and the religious environment have created a need for new organizations to support the integration of faith and health. Both fueled by emerging trends and responding to needs as they develop, these organizations reflect the diverse components of the faith and health ministry movement and have contributed to professional dialogue, research, education, and program development. Taken together they help shape a national and, to a lesser degree, international infrastructure to support the growth of health ministries.

Two groups have been integral to the development of congregationally based health ministries. The International Parish Nurse Resource Center (IPNRC) began in 1985 at Lutheran General Hospital in Park Ridge, Illinois, to provide resources and training for the development of parish nursing. The IPNRC is now with the Deaconess Foundation in St. Louis. It is a leader in parish nurse education, training, research, and support, providing an annual conference and parish nurse curriculum. The Health Ministries Association (HMA) is an interdisciplinary and interfaith group with local chapters around the country and an annual conference. HMA started in 1989 as the professional membership organization for persons serving in health ministries. Its practice and education committee wrote the parish nurse standards of practice, approved by the American Nurses Association in 1998. HMA, with a strong and growing membership, has emerged as a leader in this field.

The organization provides a valuable forum for interdisciplinary discussion about health ministries.

Two other groups have been at the forefront in recognizing the potential of faith and health partnerships to positively influence the health of communities. The Interfaith Health Program (IHP) of Emory University in Atlanta, Georgia, has brought resources to the development of health ministry through exploring issues of faith and health in national programs, conferences, and publications since 1992. IHP has been responsible for bringing the dialogue on faith and health to the wider religious community and to the public health community. The second group is the Caucus on Public Health and the Faith Community of the American Public Health Association, formed in 1996. The caucus provides a vehicle for disseminating research and best practice experiences in faith and health partnerships, and reflects the value the public health community places on working with the religious community.

PRACTICAL APPLICATION

You do not need to be a church historian to engage a congregation in promoting health. However, recognizing the historic context that frames the experience of ministry for today's churches provides an opportunity to make connections with past, present, and future ministries. As churches develop authentic health ministries today it is crucial to remind them that the restoration of health through healing was significant to the early church and periodically throughout history—a perspective that some churches may find inspiring for developing health ministries. An appreciation of the unique history of each congregation, and their denomination if so affiliated, related to health contributes to developing health ministries congruent with their ethos. In addition to the historic context, the contemporary social milieu shapes opportunities for health ministries and influences the response of individuals and communities. Each local congregation will interact with these broad contextual factors and their own local perspective to develop health ministries uniquely suited to their congregational culture.

Individual congregations and denominations have their own distinct cultures shaped by their shared values and beliefs. Congregations both influence and are influenced by the larger culture within which they exist. This is particularly evident with the concept of health ministry. Broader issues in American society affect how the concept of health ministry has emerged in dialogue and in practice within religious and professional groups. Conversely, how health ministry has developed affects society as well. Health ministry is a concept whose emergence is clearly associated with a particular point in history. There would be no need for wholistic health if Western thought had not separated body, mind, and spirit. It would be redundant, because the understanding of wholistic would be implicit in health. There would be no need for health ministry as a distinct response if the Church had never minimized its responsibility to heal, because promoting health would be integral to the concept of ministry.

QUESTIONS FOR REFLECTION

1. Does this congregation and its denomination, if so affiliated, have a history of involvement in issues of health? Healing? Medical missions?

2. Are there any significant events or issues in the history of this congregation or in the local and regional community that would influence the development or expansion of ministries of health?

3. Would understanding the historical context for the church's role in health and healing influence the credibility of ministries of health for this congregation? Why or why not?

4. What local or regional factors are influencing contemporary interest in health ministries in your community?

IDEAS FOR CONGREGATIONAL ENGAGEMENT

1. What resources, such as archives, publications, or people, are available for learning about the history of this congregation?

2. Talk about the church's history with long-time members, being particularly attentive to matters that might influence contemporary health ministries.

4

UNDERSTANDING CONGREGATIONAL CULTURE

A Key to Health Ministries

Around the country, churches are responding to the growing interest in the relationship between faith and health. Redwood Covenant Church in Santa Rosa, California, has a holistic model of health ministry; St. Stanislaus Kostka Church in Bay City, Michigan, has a health ministry cabinet building on congregational strengths; Peace Lutheran Church in Lombard, Illinois, has a Center for Healing; and Trinity United Methodist Church in Beaver Dam, Wisconsin, collaborated to develop Church Health Services with other congregations and community partners. All of these churches share an interest in promoting health, but each chose to do so in a way uniquely suited to their congregation and surrounding community. The distinctive culture of each congregation and their health ministry setting are reflected in these varied approaches to health ministry.

ELEMENTS OF CONGREGATIONAL CULTURE

Culture is "the learned, shared, and transmitted values, beliefs, norms and lifeways of a particular group that guide their thinking, decisions and actions in patterned ways."[1] While ethnicity—a culture to which one is born—is the most common perception of culture, the qualities of cultures are found in many groups of choice, including organizations, professions, and congregations. A congregation is a group of people who share religious values, rituals, experiences, language, and beliefs, all shaping behavior and responses to each other and the outside world. This distinctive culture and local theology develop in response to the congregation's unique setting, as well as to their understanding of Christian tradition, shaping what is socially and pastorally possible for that church.[2] While all Christian congregations share the belief that Jesus is God's Son, there is tremendous diversity in how this belief is lived out in the congregation and the community.[3]

Congregations have four qualities that distinguish them as local cultures[4] and shape the possibilities for promoting health. First, congregations consist of a group of people who may be diverse or homogeneous. The nature of the group will shape both the need for health ministries and the resources available for their development. Second, congregations engage in regular, intentional gathering, which will provide both the context and opportunities for health ministry activities. Third, congregations gather for the purpose of corporate worship. As a central activity in congregational life, worship provides an opportunity to articulate and experience the connections between faith and health. Finally, congregations gather to worship in a particular place. This physical setting shapes congregational life and provides opportunities for health ministry. Understanding the unique expression of these four qualities can reveal how health ministries might be integrated into a particular congregation.

AN EXAMPLE: REDWOOD COVENANT CHURCH

The health ministry of Redwood Covenant Church in Santa Rosa, California, is a reflection of both the culture of the congregation and the culture of the surrounding community. As a relatively new church of twenty-five years, a celebratory style of worship reflects the congregation's culture and is demonstrated in the sanctuary's name of Celebration Hall. People are attracted to the church by the great music and charismatic preacher. The church's health ministry is shaped by the theological perspective of the congregation's evangelical tradition that emphasizes relationship with Christ leading to wholeness and healing as part of their health ministry.

Sonoma County in California is characterized by a strong New Age influence that reflects a search for spirituality as well as a hunger for intimacy and depth. Redwood Covenant's spiritual component in their Christ-centered health ministries reaches out to this New Age interest in spirituality. Healing, as the restoration of health, is emphasized in recognition of the woundedness many bring to the church. Redwood Covenant is known in the community as a church that openly welcomes hurting people. Anyone can go there and be accepted.

Responding to the unique context of this congregation, the church's ministry of health is a crucial component of Journey, a comprehensive ministry of Christ-centered spirituality, healing, and wholeness, which addresses a range of spiritual and psychological issues. Recognizing the interrelationships between body, mind, and spirit, the Journey ministry provides divorce care and other support groups. An active visitation ministry for those who are ill is also part of the holistic approach to health ministry. Joan Scarborough, the director of the health ministry, explains this holistic approach. "I don't want to just fix somebody and put on band aids. When we started the health ministry we did blood pressure checks and blood drives. Now I want to get at root causes that are not physical. Forgiveness is a root cause of many physical problems. When people feel forgiven I've seen their countenance change."

FACTORS INFLUENCING CONGREGATIONAL CULTURE

As can be seen from this example, religious beliefs, membership demographics, and the surrounding community all influence congregational culture and the formation of health ministries. Practically, the religious beliefs of the congregation are lived out through worship, rituals, traditions, and ministry activities. Conceptually, heritage, denominational loyalty, and religious authority reflect religious beliefs that shape congregational culture. "Some congregations are anchored in their accumulated past of faith practices, culture, and tradition. Others emphasize a denominational identity. Still others see their understanding of religious authority as a unifying force."[5] If Christian tradition is a unifying factor, church members may find a discussion of the history of the church in health and healing compelling. If denominational loyalty is strong, sharing health ministry resources developed by the denomination may generate interest in health ministries. Scripture is a source of religious authority for all Christians, although its primacy varies among churches. Studying the biblical stories of healing can draw on the religious authority of scripture in developing ministries of health. The religious authority of the Holy Spirit is also significant to some churches. For them, discerning the guidance of the Holy Spirit in the area of health ministry may be important.[6]

In addition to shared religious beliefs, the demographics of the membership affect congregational culture and the possibilities for health ministry. Factors such as ethnicity, age, gender, education, socioeconomic status, and the size of the congregation both reflect and influence congregational culture. Consider ethnicity. Not only does the congregation have a culture, but each member of the congregation comes from his or her own ethnic culture that informs how that person participates in the life and ministry of the church. Understanding ethnic cultures within the congregation may provide insight for developing health ministries. Similarly, age, gender balance, and family constitution will influence both the culture of the congregation and the opportunities for health ministry. Congregations with clusters by age groups will have different health issues. For example, aging congregations are likely to experience issues with chronic illness, disability, and death. Congregations with a preponderance of families with children will likely experience issues regarding parenting, safety, and human development.

Educational levels of members will influence the approach to health ministry. In a congregation with an average education level of high school or less, communicating information orally may be more desirable and reading levels of written materials will need to be at an appropriate level. In these churches, training lay people in basic health education can make health information more accessible. In a well-educated congregation, written communication may be preferred and health information should also be provided at an appropriate level. Professional credentials of health ministry leadership may be important.

Socioeconomic status is closely related to education. It will be reflected in members' health issues and will influence the assets and resources available for developing health ministries. For example, in a congregation with a low average income, access to health care may be a significant issue and advocacy regarding health concerns an appropriate response. In a congregation with a high average income, stress from demanding lifestyles may be a concern, and workshops on stress management an appropriate response.

Subcultures within the congregation can be shaped around any of these demographic factors or by special interest groups. No congregation is culturally uniform. Groups that gather together frequently have the potential to be subcultures, and can significantly influence congregational life. In many churches the choir is a special interest group that has its own subculture. The caring connections often found in church groups may indirectly promote health through providing social support and can also be potential partners in health ministry.

Taken together, these demographic characteristics of a congregation describe a group whose size will impact congregational life. A large congregation may have more financial and staff resources, as well as subcultures. Being large may necessitate complex processes for decision making. A small congregation may have fewer financial resources yet be rich in social capital. A quick response may be possible as needs and interests arise.[7] When considering health ministries, a large congregation may have more health professionals willing to participate and a larger budget to hire a health minister. Yet, a small congregation with its relational strength might be able to initiate a health ministry more quickly.

Whether large or small, congregations engage in regular, intentional gathering. Patterns of gathering both influence and reflect the culture of the congregation, providing the setting and opportunities for health ministry activities. Gathering frequently during the week facilitates close relationships and provides potential opportunities for health ministry activities.

Gathering only on Sunday can create a looser sense of affiliation and generate competition among ministry activities.

Consider this example from a church with which I worked whose membership was drawn from a wide geographic area and who primarily gathered on Sunday. This particular Sunday was designated for health awareness. The worship service included a liturgy written by the parish nurse and a sermon on health. It also included readings and music in Spanish because it was also Hispanic awareness Sunday. In addition, a visiting group of Masons in full regalia were recognized during the service. After church, people could choose from a health discussion and flu shots or a Mexican lunch. With only fifty-two Sundays in a year, there is no way that health ministry programs will not compete with other activities in a busy church.

Congregations gather in a particular place on Sundays and throughout the week. They are physically located in an urban, rural, or suburban neighborhood that influences congregational life both directly and indirectly. The setting also creates opportunities for health ministry. Whether in the city, suburbs, or country, congregations connect to their neighborhoods in different ways. Some churches are integrally involved in their neighborhoods and others only use their neighborhood as a location. Whether membership is drawn from long distances or within walking distance, as in a "parish" church, often influences neighborhood connectedness.

PERSPECTIVES ON UNDERSTANDING CONGREGATIONAL CULTURE

Relationships with the neighborhood are influenced by the self-image of the congregation and the understanding of their mission. The congregation's perception of itself in relationship to members, the neighborhood, and the world will influence its ministries in general and its health ministries in particular. These dynamics can be discerned with conceptual tools from the field of congregational studies. One framework for understanding can be found in the work of Carl Dudley and Sally Johnson, whose five congregational self-images offer one way to understand congregations.[8]

The survivor church is the first self-image. It reacts repeatedly to crises and overwhelming situations. The leadership within survivor churches may be burned out by crises, though these crises may generate support from the congregation. Still, a survivor church is not likely to have the energy or resources to develop health ministry programs, even though it might rescue particular individuals in need.

The prophet church is the second self-image. It takes on causes, has leaders with vision and a dramatic style, and has members active in mission. A prophet church might be interested in developing a health ministry that takes on health care system issues, such as the lack of universal health insurance or systemic concerns related to persons with AIDS.

The pillar church is the third self-image. It has a strong sense of civic responsibility to a specific community. These churches have professionally trained leadership. Their typically large membership creates a lower sense of intimacy and involvement in decision making. A pillar church is likely to be interested in expansive health ministry programs such as faith and health partnerships to improve the health of the community.

The pilgrim church is the fourth self-image, characterized by caring for a specific ethnic or cultural group. Shaped by the immigrant experience, leadership in this church is characterized by traditional values associated with the ethnic or cultural group. There is a strong sense of history and involvement in social ministry. The health ministry of a pilgrim church might assist members to establish themselves in American society by helping people access available health resources and by providing health education and information about health career opportunities.

Finally, the servant church supports persons in need. Leaders are caregivers and the membership is a gathering of individuals with low group cohesiveness. A servant church would want its health ministry to help members and neighbors with greatest need. A health ministry might be shaped around individual health concerns rather than programs.

In addition to self-images, mission orientation provides another perspective for understanding congregations' relationships with their neighborhood and the world. Roozen, McKinney, and Carroll offer the following four congregational mission orientations.[9]

Congregations with a sanctuary orientation perceive their mission as providing a safe haven in the community. Making space available for health promotion programs might be a meaningful health ministry for this church.

A congregation with an evangelistic orientation sees their mission as changing the world through seeking converts. This church might find an adult education class exploring the relationships between religious faith and personal health a meaningful health ministry.

Congregations with a civic orientation want to promote and preserve what is good in this world. This church might find partnerships to improve community health a meaningful health ministry.

Finally, relieving suffering and injustice through changing world structures is the concern of an activist congregation. A church with this orientation might find addressing issues of world health through advocacy and missions a meaningful health ministry.

Neither self-images nor mission orientations are meant to be an exhaustive or mutually exclusive way to understand churches. They identify a tendency in group attitude, as does the Myer's Briggs personality typology for individuals. How useful these perspectives are depends on their ability to enhance our understanding of a congregation. What is important is to recognize that every church has a way of looking at the world that reflects their values and beliefs and shapes how a vision for health might be expressed in church life.

GATHERING INFORMATION ON CONGREGATIONAL CULTURE

Understanding self-image, mission orientation, and congregational culture requires an intentional process of reflection and gathering information, whether you are a church member or an outsider. You need to "dwell with" the congregation before jumping into health ministry activities and programs. Enthusiastic new health ministers can easily be tempted to emphasize programs, activities, and doing at the expense of being with the congregation and growing in an understanding of congregational culture. Many a person has approached starting a health ministry with vigor and enthusiasm, anxious to provide programs he or she perceives as needed by the church, only to receive a lukewarm response to his or her efforts. This frustration may be avoided by laying an appropriate foundation for health ministries that acknowledges the particularity of the individual congregation as reflected in its culture and builds on its unique strengths and assets. Laying a firm foundation takes time.

To begin the process of engaging a congregation in ministries of health, start by looking at the church as a novice trying to learn a new system. Reflect on your personal cultural assumptions about churches and health ministry. What preconceived ideas do you bring? Involve others in learning about the congregation's culture. Not only do health ministry leaders need to understand how health might fit into church life, but the congregation needs to understand as well. Talk with church members to comprehend the meaning of behavior, being mindful that our questions both reveal and shape the information received. Avoid questions that can be answered by yes or no. Instead ask open-ended questions, such as "How does this church care for its members?"

There is also much that can be learned through observation. Many cultural meanings are taken for granted in churches, meanings expressed implicitly through stories, symbols, rituals, and behavior.[10] Participant observation is a useful technique for learning about these implicit dimensions of culture. Everyone learns about his or her own culture through observation, participation, and asking questions. As a participant observer, be highly attentive as you observe and ask questions about cultural meanings of others, and of yourself,[11] such as, "What is really happening here?" and "Why is this happening at the church?"

In reality, it is impossible to purely observe group behavior. Simply by virtue of your presence, you participate. This is particularly true when learning about a congregation where worship is a major cultural event. Even so, stepping back and observing even while participating can reveal valuable insights. As a health minister you will need to learn and reflect on two levels. First, you will want to understand congregational culture in general. Second, you will want to recognize the foundations on which health ministries can be built. Although understanding culture can be a means in itself because it is a very interesting thing to do, in this case it is a means to an end.

Every congregation has formal and informal patterns of communication. Identifying these patterns of verbal and written communication will not only provide cultural information but also identify possibilities for disseminating health ministry information. Some congregations rely heavily on written tradition and others on oral tradition. If a congregation has a written tradition, learn what can be read to help understand the congregation and identify the written venues available for communicating health information. If the congregation has an oral tradition, find the most knowledgeable members and learn how information is shared. Beyond oral and written traditions, some congregations utilize technology for communication, in which case websites and e-mail can be important resources for communicating health information.

The Congregational Assessment Guide (Appendix A) provides questions that can be used to direct participant observation. It is a cognitive map that outlines helpful areas of cultural knowledge when engaging a congregation in ministries of health. It is based on what I have found to be significant in working with congregations. You may not need to gain information in all areas, but the guide identifies key components of congregational culture that can influence health ministries. You do not have to travel down every road, but the guide can help you frame the possibilities for acquiring valuable cultural information. Your health ministry role will influence what cultural information is needed. For example, a health ministry leader serving in one congregation will need more specific cultural information than a health ministry coordinator from a local hospital recruiting churches for a health ministry network.

Consider the following important sources of information as you look for how health is, or could be, addressed. Attend worship services, paying attention to the rituals, the people, and the atmosphere. Look for and ponder the meaning of any artifacts, and/or symbols such as art work, sculpture, or items of worship. Attend social events of the congregation, paying attention to the people, the atmosphere, and the content. Identify the regularly occurring (at least once a year) events that are significant in this congregation (such as the pastor's anniversary, annual meeting, retreats, or church picnic). Attend committee meetings, particularly those that deal with issues of care for the congregation, community outreach, education, and finances. Note what issues are discussed and how decisions are made. Read written materials such as the mission statement, Sunday bulletins, newsletters, annual reports, minutes of relevant committee meetings, and documents of church history, looking to identify significant events and recurring themes. Talk with a variety of people, including clergy, church staff, church secretary, and active lay people such as members of the church's governing body, leaders of groups (i.e., women, men, and youth). Listen to the stories frequently told by members, contemplating the congregational values they reflect.

While most people seeking to engage a congregation in ministries of health will be working with an established congregation with a history, a few will be working with a new church, which may provide the unique opportunity to integrate health throughout the life of the church as it is being formed. This situation adds a different dimension to understanding congregational culture. A new church plant will be defining its emerging culture, while an established congregation will have many people and events from the past that continue to influence the church today. A church plant may be heavily shaped by the strengths, needs, and resources of individual members.

While new, it still emerges from a particular heritage for a particular reason. Understanding the context that has shaped and is shaping the new church will be of particular importance when forming ministries of health.

IMPLICATIONS FOR MINISTRIES OF HEALTH

Whether working with a new or an established church to promote health, the culture of the congregation is not the only culture that must be understood. As health ministry has emerged in contemporary society, it has done so in response to varied cultural influences. Health ministry is inherently cross-cultural, bridging the professional cultures of health and ministry as well as the organizational cultures of congregations and health care, creating something that neither could accomplish alone. When the resources of health and ministry are joined, building on the strength of each perspective, there are abundant opportunities to promote health. Challenges also proliferate as shared values, beliefs, and understandings are sought between the two professional cultures.

Health ministry combines an understanding of health with an understanding of ministry, joining elements from the health care system and the congregation. Hospitals and churches operate from different assumptions. Consider some of the following qualities I have identified from my work with hospitals and congregations that characterize the culture of health care and the culture of the congregation. The contrasts demonstrate some health ministry challenges. Keep in mind that while these are offered as general tendencies, there is wide variation among both health care systems and congregations.

The following dominant patterns characterize the culture of health care, reflecting the general values and beliefs of that organizational culture. The decision-making process in health care resides in the administrative structure, which is equipped for making quick decisions and delegating the organization's significant resources. Health care organizations are bureaucratic and have many paid employees. A hospital operates twenty-four hours a day, seven days a week. The organizational style is formal and bureaucratic. Cure is a dominant value. Numbers served and the financial bottom line shape the measure of success. Medicine with its scientific and technological emphasis is the dominant language spoken in the culture of health care. Whether or not a health ministry is hospital sponsored, the health professionals serving in the church bring the mindset of health care.

Contrast this with the dominant patterns that characterize congregations and that reflect the general values and beliefs of a congregation's organizational culture. The decision-making process in congregations is widely variable and influenced by size, ethnicity, congregational leadership, and polity. Compared to health care, congregations make decisions slowly. Churches rely heavily on volunteers and typically have few paid staff. The schedule of the church is organized around Sundays as the primary gathering time with other evening activities during the week. The prevalent organizational style is informal. Healing, in a holistic rather than a purely physical sense, is a dominant value. Membership numbers and faithfulness to mission are measures of success. Practical theology is the dominant language in the culture of the congregation.

Consider the potential challenge when these two diverse cultures work together. For example, in my experience as a health ministry coordinator for a large academic medical center, a legal agreement was needed to clarify the relationship between the hospital and the congregation. Churches typically do not prepare legal agreements when engaging in a partnership, yet legal agreements are standard for hospitals. This procedure, which was based on the hospital's values and beliefs, required interpretation and explanation for the congregations.

In addition to hospitals, there are a growing number of public health initiatives working with congregations. The distinctiveness of the pubic health perspective as it interfaces with the church will be discussed in chapter 7.

Anyone working to engage congregations in ministries of health needs to bridge the cultures of health care and the culture of ministry. There is a sense in which you need to be bilingual—able to understand both the language of the church and the language of health as a shared language of health ministry emerges.[12] Through understanding congregational culture, a ministry of health can be developed that is consistent with the values, beliefs, resources, capabilities, and needs of the congregation. Members need to be engaged in uncovering their significant values and beliefs in order to discern appropriate health ministries. Taking time to learn how a congregation works and what it values will create a sense of mutuality and provide credibility to the health ministry. For health ministry coordinators, understanding congregational culture will facilitate connecting faith and health conceptually and practically as an appropriate health ministry program for the wider community is developed.

The significance of understanding culture has been documented in many health care settings.[13] Cultural understanding enables health and ministry professionals to care for others in meaningful and effective ways. This same concept extends to the congregation when health and ministry professionals collaborate to promote health, healing, and wholeness. Health ministries will "fit" in the church when they are consistent with the culture of the congregation and members understand why their congregation should be involved in health promotion—as at Redwood Covenant. If health ministry is not congruent with the congregational culture there will be frustration and the ministry will not be effective. The significance of cultural understanding for health ministries needs to be recognized to build the church's capacity to positively influence the health of individuals, families, congregations, and communities.

QUESTIONS FOR REFLECTION

1. What sources of information are available for understanding the culture of this congregation as it relates to health ministries?

2. What questions about this congregation do you bring to this process?

3. How might your own experience of church influence your understanding of the culture of this congregation?

4. What are the sources of religious authority for this congregation and how might those be used in developing ministries of health?

IDEAS FOR CONGREGATIONAL ENGAGEMENT

1. Look over the Congregational Assessment Guide (Appendix A) and, in cooperation with others interested in health ministries, begin gathering information.

2. If this church is affiliated with a denomination, learn about any denominational resources for health ministries and evaluate their suitability for your congregation.

3. Read *Studying Congregations* by Nancy Ammerman, Jackson Carroll, Carl Dudley, and William McKinney to gain further insight into congregational culture.

5

BUILDING THE
CONGREGATION'S CAPACITY
TO PROMOTE HEALTH

E ach congregation has strengths within their culture that
can be used to promote health. They also have health related needs. An awareness of both strengths and needs is
necessary to health ministries, yet which is emphasized will
drastically influence the character of health ministries. In community development this is referred to as the "outside in" or
the "inside out" approach. The old "outside in" paradigm identified problems that could be solved by professionals through
needs assessments. Health ministers may similarly be tempted
to look at the needs and problems of the congregation they can
address professionally. Consider instead the contemporary "inside out" community development paradigm that looks for
community strengths and assets. These individual and organizational resources are then utilized to build the capacity of the
community to solve their own problems. This approach is
known as assets-based community development (ABCD).[1]

The concepts of ABCD can be used in health ministries on
the individual, congregational, or community level. Health concerns addressed with individuals or groups should be self-defined, hence the significance of really listening to people. On the
congregational level, understanding the culture and working

with a health ministry cabinet are important. Lone ranger health ministers will run into problems. Health ministries need to engage as much of the congregation as possible to be most effective. Each church member has gifts he or she can offer. Some of these gifts can be used for ministries of health. The community (in this case the congregation) will be its healthiest when all the gifts of all of the members are fully utilized.[2]

AN EXAMPLE: ST. STANISLAUS KOSTKA CHURCH

Consider what St. Stanislaus Kostka Church, affectionately referred to as St. Stan's, learned about working with strengths. A large Catholic parish in Bay City, Michigan, their health ministry began after a member completed a parish nurse training program. She gathered together an informal health ministry cabinet and for several years random health ministry programs were provided with a variable response. Their health ministry was transformed to a new level when the approach changed to understanding the culture, values, and strengths of the parish in order to develop an effective and meaningful ministry of health. After a thorough assessment of the parish culture by Carol Vos, parish nurse, the following strengths were identified and used to transform their ministry of health.

The ability to come together to pray and worship is a primary strength of St. Stan's. The Light Weigh program, a Catholic based weight loss program, combining prayer and worship life with Catholic values to help individuals achieve a healthy weight, is one creative way this strength has been used. The health ministry cabinet saw an opportunity to use their strength in prayer and worship to provide needed health education.

An additional strength is the ability to convene in community, reflected in the many ways this parish gathers together and enjoys fellowship. Building on this strength, and recognizing the health promoting benefits of connecting with others, the health ministry cabinet created the Holy Grounds Café, which convenes once a month, providing health screenings and healthy foods in an atmosphere of fellowship. After trying several different programming approaches, the health ministry cabinet recognized the need to provide programming when people were already congregating, as in the senior citizen's group, or give them a reason to congregate, as in the Holy Grounds Café.

Accompanying each other along life's journey is also a strength of St. Stan's. The health cabinet has built on this historic strength of the parish community by encouraging informal care among the members. Cards are sent and meals provided during times of illness or special need. This caring connection is an informal part of community life that permeates the whole parish and is not dependent on staff leadership.

Numerous gifted members who can support ministries of health are one of St. Stan's significant assets. Recognizing this valuable social capital, the health ministry cabinet has enlisted many volunteers. Nurses, nursing assistants, physical therapists, occupational therapists, and interested lay people have all contributed their gifts. Acknowledging the significance of using the gifts of the membership, the health ministry cabinet has used a recommitment drive to help recognize the contributions of this group. Having strengthened the ministry of health in ways that are congruent with the culture of St. Stan's, the parish is now ready to consider hiring a full-time health minister to work with the health ministry cabinet.

St. Stan's is affiliated with the Saginaw Valley State University parish nurse program, based on the ABCD conceptual framework. Each parish nurse identifies his or her personal assets and gifts as well as the strengths and assets of the community in which each works. This framework helps the parish nurse work with the congregation to build the capacity to address areas of concern rather than focus on problems and deficits.

COMMUNITY DEVELOPMENT PRINCIPLES IN HEALTH MINISTRIES

Other churches can learn from community development and the example of St. Stan's. It has been common in the helping professions to focus on perceived needs and deficits of the other, be it an individual, a family, or a community. And quite often it is a need that brings the other to our attention as pastor or health professional. Yet, to respond effectively strengths need to be recognized as well as the problem defined. Thinking about strengths and assets rather than needs and problems is similar to looking at a cup as half full rather than half empty. While the facts remain the same, the perception affects the meaning given to the situation and affects the response.[3] One revealing exercise I have students do that demonstrates these perceptual differences is to first list the problems of their congregation and community and then the strengths. Frequently you can not tell they are talking about the same group.

While community development comes from a secular perspective, churches would find it consistent with the scriptural concept of spiritual gifts found in 1 Corinthians chapter 12. Everyone has gifts that can contribute to the good of the whole. Similarly, everyone in the congregation can make a contribution to health ministries. People who are in need can also provide assistance to others. An example comes from a church I used to attend. There was a young man with chronic mental illness who lived in a nearby halfway house. Periodically he required assistance from the church, and yet he was also able to serve. He became the designated dishwasher for church meals, which gave him a way to serve and also a small income. This was good for his health.

LIMITS OF CHARITY

In the church, emphasizing needs and problems leads to acts of charity. While everyone can use some help, this approach does little to address the root issues of health problems. Charity may make the person offering it feel better and it may address an immediate need, but it does not address the real problem. Responding to the justice issues behind the need for charity is more challenging and complex, but is also more likely to eliminate the problem.[4] In *The Careless Society*, John McKnight adds another perspective to the limits of charity.[5] He talks about how caring has been professionalized to the extent that communities have been disempowered. Social service agencies and institutions now provide professional care that families and communities used to provide informally, such as caring for the mentally ill or persons who are homeless. "Helping" both people and communities can be disabling when solving the problems becomes someone else's responsibility.

Many churches start their health ministries from a desire to help persons in need. This approach based on compassion and mercy provides a valuable, immediate service. Other churches will choose to take on issues of justice to correct the root issues of health problems in their health ministries. For example, a church concerned about the issue of access to health care may develop a free clinic and provide a much needed service, as happened with Church Health Services discussed in chapter 7. Another response to the same problem addressing root causes would be working for national policy change to ensure universal, affordable health care. Both approaches are needed. One deals with short-term issues and one addresses long-term issues. The challenge for the health ministry leader is to discern in collaboration with others the appropriate response for their particular congregation.

Speaking to the concerns of the congregation, community, or individual should take priority in any health ministry. This may or may not be what you as a pastor or health professional believe should be the primary concern. Individual and community capacity grows when people are successful in prioritizing and addressing self-defined problems. The following statement attributed to Paul Tillich is a good reminder when developing health ministries: The fatal pedagogical error is to throw answers, like stones, at the heads of those who have not yet asked the questions.

CONGREGATIONAL STRENGTHS

What can congregations bring to a transforming vision of health? Certainly their unique strengths that distinguish them from other community groups provide new possibilities for ministries of health. Gary Gunderson has been a leader in describing the possibilities for congregations to enhance the health of their communities. In his book *Deeply Woven Roots*, he identifies eight strengths of congregations; the strength to accompany, to convene, to connect, to tell stories, to give sanctuary, to bless, to pray, and to endure.[6] You will recognize that St. Stan's used this conceptual framework in their health ministry. Consider how these congregational strengths can be used in ministries of health to transform the health of communities.

Strength to Accompany

Being in relationship with others is one of the fundamental components of church life. Congregations are groups of people that accompany each other throughout life's journeys. In ministries of health when members intentionally accompany each other through life's journeys of health and illness, the congregation uses its strength to accompany. Practically, churches do this through the social support of small groups or hospital visitation.

Strength to Convene

Gathering together is part of being a church. This ability to bring people together can be extended to the community as the relationships developed over time enable the church to bring people together around issues of mutual concern. Churches can draw on their moral authority in their efforts to convene. In addition to the relational resources needed to bring people together, churches also have the space for hosting groups. In ministries of health, when folks are brought together for a support group, or to address concerns about the health of the community, the congregation uses its strength to convene.

Strength to Connect

Congregations have the ability to create links across people, assets, knowledge, and power in the community, creating a rich source of social capital. Congregations as an organization connect with their communities and their members provide additional links to a range of resources. In ministries of health when the church engages in a faith and health partnership or when individuals are connected to available health and social resources, the congregation uses its strength to connect. Health advocacy for individuals or communities creates connections.

Strength to Tell Stories

The stories we tell are as important as what actually happened. Telling stories both creates and interprets meaning for individuals or for groups. One assignment I give my students is to identify the congregational stories frequently repeated as one way of understanding self-image, values, and cultural myths. Telling communal stories and listening to the stories of individuals are both health promoting things that congregations do.

Strength to Give Sanctuary

The physical space of a congregation is a strength. In order to gather together, groups need a place, and for congregations that is their sanctuary, rich with symbols that communicate meaning. It may also include a fellowship hall, Sunday school classrooms, or a gym. This physical space is an asset that can be shared with others. When congregations share their building for exercise programs, weight loss programs, and twelve-step programs, they promote the health of their community.

Strength to Bless

Congregations have the strength to bless others through words of love, acts of welcome, and walking with those who are hurting. Like Jacob wrestling with God in Genesis 32:22–30, humans long to be blessed and affirmed by others. Congregations have the potential to include and to exclude people. When people are welcomed into the fellowship of a congregation and warmly included, the congregation can have a positive influence on health.

Strength to Pray

Praying together is a distinguishing characteristic and strength of congregations. Prayer is a regular activity of both individuals and the community of faith, allowing the opportunity to share concerns and burdens while drawing upon God's resources. When congregations pray for each other and their community, they have the potential to positively influence health.

Strength to Endure

Congregations do not usually change quickly. They are largely volunteer associations that take time to change and thus offer stability for their members and their community. The intergenerational nature of congregations provides a unique opportunity for interaction and also reflects their durability. Congregations provide a sense of history within their communities that contributes to their credibility that can be used to promote community health. While new churches will begin without a long-standing history in their communities, they will, by extension with the tradition of churches throughout the centuries, have the expectation of endurance that will eventually lead to a shared history with the community.

Looking practically at the strengths of congregations, Kretzmann and McKnight identify personnel, space and facilities, materials and equipment, and expertise as assets that can be used to build communities.[7] Churches are a good source of volunteers. Their space, facilities, and equipment can potentially be used for a wide range of community activities. Congregations have expertise in community knowledge and the power of moral authority. They have potential economic power to generate funds for community endeavors.

Another perspective on congregational strengths relevant to health ministries is offered by Rev. Granger Westberg, parish nursing visionary.

> Churches are to be found everywhere, out in neighborhoods where people live—urban, suburban, rural—and their buildings are largely unused during the weekdays. Churches have a long history of serving their communities through social activities and continuing education programs. Churches symbolize our need to take seriously the problems of the human spirit, which are so often related to the causes of illness. Churches provide a remarkable reservoir of dedicated people who are willing to volunteer their services to assist in humanitarian endeavors. Church members have a growing appreciation for the opportunity to model, in their own church buildings, the need for cooperation between scientific medicine and religious faith.[8]

Whatever the perspective, it is clear that congregations have significant strengths that can be used to promote health. In addition to those qualities shared by congregations in general, each church will have its own unique assets. As an important part of every community, congregations can be effective partners in improving the health of individuals, families, and communities through the appropriate use of their moral authority, the resources of religious beliefs and their credibility as a community organization.

IDENTIFYING CONGREGATIONAL AND COMMUNITY STRENGTHS

Recognizing that all congregations have strengths, how do you identify the strengths of a particular church? You can begin by exploring the members' perceptions of what the church does best, and the ministries perceived to be most effective. Identify to what people willingly give their money and their time. This is one indication of values and also of congregational strength. If there are always plenty of people to serve as Sunday school teachers, or to cook for a church potluck, that is an area of strength.

Communities as well as congregations have strengths that can be used to develop health ministries. Hospitals, neighborhood associations, educational institutions, businesses, or social service agencies are all community assets and potential partners for health ministries. In addition, all communities have "social capital," the web of human relationships that makes things happen. Communities with limited economic and educational resources may still be rich in social relationships. Social capital can be a priceless resource for health ministries as it connects people addressing mutual concerns. The potential for building on community strengths to develop faith and health partnerships will be discussed more fully in chapter 7.

HEALTH ASSESSMENT OF THE CONGREGATION AND COMMUNITY

Although building on strengths is the emphasis in ABCD, the purpose of this approach is to address issues of concern to the congregation or community. One way to identify health concerns is a survey. Whether this is appropriate will depend on the preferred style of sharing information in your congregation. You can also gather information through informal and formal conversations with church members and key leaders, as well as through observations. If your congregation has a strong oral tradition, conversation is likely to be more informative than a written survey.

Four simple questions asked of a variety of individuals and/or church groups may provide the basic information needed.

1. What is your greatest concern about your health?
2. Is there anything about health that you would be interested in learning?
3. How do you think this church might help you and other members to be healthy?
4. What might you be able to contribute to a health ministry in this congregation?

If a survey of health interests would be appropriate for your congregation,[9] and it certainly is not for all congregations, think about how to get the best response. You will get the most replies if time is allotted during a worship service or other church event to complete the survey. To do this effectively, the purpose of the survey and how it will be used needs to be shared with the group. Asking only information you need and will make use of is another important principle. Also, do not ask unnecessary personal information, and include the opportunity for people to identify what they could contribute to a health ministry as well as identifying health concerns.

Identifying the health concerns of the community can be approached in a manner similar to that used with a congregation with some modifications. Surveys can be used if there are adequate human resources. However, using a survey with a community creates a logistical challenge in accessing a representative sample. Statistical information tabulated by local departments of health is a resource available for identifying community health problems not available for congregations. This information will identify the incidence of certain diseases and causes of death. It will not tell you if the community is concerned about those diseases. For example, a high rate of deaths from cancer does not necessarily mean this is the top health concern for the community. They may be more concerned about community safety. The only way to know is to ask and listen.

Talking with community members, groups, and key leaders is a productive way to gather information. Some useful questions developed by the Center for Health Professions include:[10]

1. What creates and sustains health in the community?
2. What are the health issues as defined by residents?
3. What are the health assets as defined by residents?
4. How do residents perceive the health of their community?

Whether addressing health concerns in the congregation or the community, the group toward which services are directed must be included in planning. For example, if a need is perceived for addressing health concerns of senior citizens, persons who are elderly need to be involved in developing the program from the beginning. Their insight should be sought on topics of interest, and how programs or services should be provided. Assuming what other people need is problematic. It is possible to guess correctly, but more often you will be frustrated by effort put into a health ministry program that was well-intentioned but incompletely planned.

Churches are community organizations with strengths that can be enlisted to promote the health of their members, as seen in the story of St. Stanislaus Kostka Church. For health ministries to be most effective, they need to have significant investment from church members who will provide the long-term support through their participation as volunteers, program participants, and financial supporters. This being done, congregations can build on their strengths to reach out to their neighborhood to transform community as well as congregational health.

QUESTIONS FOR REFLECTION

1. Can you think of examples from your own professional background or personal experience when it makes a difference to look at strengths and assets as opposed to needs and problems?

2. Congregations are unique and located in diverse communities. How might the concepts of assets based community development apply to your particular situation?

3. What is one dominant strength of your congregation? How could that strength be incorporated into health ministries?

IDEAS FOR CONGREGATIONAL ENGAGEMENT

1. Discuss with church members:
   – The needs of the congregation
   – The needs of the surrounding community
   – The assets and strengths of the congregation
   – The assets and strengths of the community
   – Any differences between the perspective of needs and assets/strengths

2. In consultation with church leadership, identify key people in the church who could be part of a health ministry leadership team

3. Discuss with the pastor and/or appropriate church leaders the best way to identify the congregations' interests and concerns regarding health.

4. Read *Asset-Based Strategies for Faith Communities* by Susan Rans and Hilary Altman.

6

THE CHURCH AND HEALTHY COMMUNITIES[1]

I ndividualism is both a strength and a weakness of American culture. We believe in a land of individual opportunity; with sufficient effort all can pull themselves up by the bootstraps. So it should not be surprising that our health care system is also individualistic. The vast majority of national health care dollars go to develop and provide treatments for individuals who are sick. A much smaller proportion of our national resources goes into promoting health and preventing disease through public health efforts in our communities.[2] This emphasis has been mirrored in our churches, which are quick to rally around an ill member, offering prayer, food, and practical assistance. However, churches have yet to fully realize their potential to promote health, prevent illness, and transform the health of communities.

With a national mindset that emphasizes individuals and illness over communities and health, it should not be surprising that many congregations first look inward, organizing their health ministries to serve individuals with health problems. Indeed, health ministers have been very effective in providing education, counseling, advocacy, and health screening to individuals. While this may be a logical place to begin, a mature health ministry needs to also look outwards toward the community, considering the broader perspective of what enables people to be well. In doing so, churches have the potential to positively influence the health of more people as their perspective is expanded to include families, groups, the congregation as a whole, and the neighborhood.[3] Churches need to do this because health is not just an individual issue. Health is also a community issue and a social responsibility.

EXPANDING THE CHURCH'S VISION

Congregations around the country are using their inherent strengths to positively influence the health of communities—through articulating the interrelationship between faith and health for individuals; through ministry with families, providing support during significant life transitions; through nurturing a health-promoting environment in congregational life; through collaborative efforts with community partners as health issues of mutual concern are addressed; and through the efforts of denominations providing health care institutions, missions, and resources for health ministries.

Health is also promoted throughout the collective life of the church, which some would easily identify in health ministry activities such as health fairs, blood pressure screenings, or health education. In addition to all of these intentional health promotion efforts, the church does much that positively influences health, even when that is not the explicit purpose, through their intrinsic health ministry. In one church, members identified this intrinsic health ministry as including a positive influence on health from the opportunity to engage in challenging experiences in a supportive environment, the positive attitude cultivated in preaching and adult education, the opportunities for spiritual growth that promoted overall well-being and mental health in particular, and belonging to a community where people would care if anything happened to you. The opportunity to engage in church activities that were pleasurable experiences was also seen as health promoting.[4]

Addressing social problems is another indirect way churches promote health. Poverty is a social problem the effects of which will be manifested in the health problems of persons who are poor. The complete solution of those health problems requires not only medical care, but social change as well. Churches with a heart for the social gospel have long been involved in social outreach and community development through ministries of housing, education, and employment. Because health has a direct relationship to social class,[5] any ministry that helps provide safe, supportive living environments and increases education and income will have a positive influence on health. When housing, education, and employment are improved in a community, the health of the individuals, families, and the neighborhood improves as well.

As the church's role in health is named and reclaimed, we need to recognize that churches play a current role in health and have a historic tradition of the same, even when there is no formal health ministry. Building on the intrinsic health ministry of the church, there is much that can be done to intentionally improve the health of individuals, families, the congregation, and the community through engaging in ministries of health.

AN EXAMPLE: PEACE LUTHERAN CHURCH

Peace Lutheran Church in Lombard, Illinois, is a good example of a church that has named and reclaimed the church's ministry of health. This is a church members describe as spirit-led, prayerful, and intentional, where no idea is too insignificant for consideration.[6] The health ministry of this large, dynamic, suburban congregation offers a good example of the importance of exploring the meaning of health when developing health ministries. Their health ministry is framed in a holistic understanding of health as exemplified in the mission statement of their health ministry, "We serve people who have spiritual, physical, emotional, and relational needs with prayer and Christ-centered care."

Reflecting their holistic perspective, they were able to identify a wide range of intrinsic ministries of health, including activities directed toward physical health, such as a cycling club, a softball team, a walk-a-thon, and a weekly homeless shelter site; activities directed towards spiritual health, such as worship, preaching, Stephen's Ministry, men's, women's, youth, and children's ministries, discipling programs, Bible study, small group Bible study, and retreats; activities meeting needs of emotional health, such as an unemployment ministry, pastoral counseling, occasional workshops, and Bible studies addressing various aspects of emotional health; and activities promoting social health, such as after worship fellowship, small group fellowship, post–mission trip fellowship, annual picnic, pig roast, and intermittent fellowship activities sponsored by the congregation. With a rich array of activities addressing the multiple dimensions of well-being, Peace has a strong foundation for health ministry.

RELIGION, SPIRITUALITY, AND PERSONAL HEALTH

Medical researchers are also aware of the positive influence of church life. The growing body of medical research on religion, spirituality, and health, documenting that people who participate frequently in religious services are healthier and live longer, has contributed to a social and cultural atmosphere conducive to addressing health concerns in the church. While many people of faith are not surprised by a positive relationship between religious participation and health, understanding the exact nature of the relationship presents a challenge for researchers. Some explanations for this effect include that healthy behavior and lifestyles are promoted by religious affiliation and membership; the effects of stress and isolation are minimized by the support offered through religious fellowship; the physiological effects of positive emotions are activated through participation in worship and prayer; religious beliefs benefit health by their similarity to health-promoting beliefs and personality styles; and hope, optimism, and positive expectation are cultivated by faith.[7]

While the common discourse created by this research contributes to interest in health ministries, the challenge of what to do with the information is problematic. Should doctors, or churches for that matter, be encouraging religious participation because it is good for health? Hardly, for such a utilitarian approach to religion would be inconsistent with Christianity and has the potential of blaming the victim when religious activities do not lead to health. Rather than using religion as a means to health, we need to know God whether we are sick or well.[8] Yet, churches can still celebrate what happens in their fellowship that creates a sense of well-being. And the fact remains that something as simple as getting members who are homebound to church, or bringing church to them, could have a positive influence on their health.

Recognizing what the church already does that promotes general well-being, as did Peace Lutheran, increases the likelihood that health will be integrated into the life of the church rather than existing as a separate program. Peace Lutheran began their intentional ministry of health in response to a collaborative relationship with a local hospital. Encouraged by the hospital to take an entire year to develop their vision and purpose for health ministries, their efforts began with a series of sermons on personal and communal health. Recognizing both the intrinsic health ministry of the church and the promise of intentional health ministries, a Center for Healing was created when the church was reorganized into four centers. A health cabinet model was chosen for the organizational structure with a staff person responsible for connecting people with resources in the community and congregation. Recognizing the need for someone with a health professional background to work with this congregation, the possibility of hiring a parish nurse is being explored. Continuing with their theme of integrating health and healing throughout the life of the church, leadership is asked to identify what is happening in their ministry area that influences health.

PROMOTING FAMILY HEALTH

Churches like Peace Lutheran are one of a variety of groups that impact health to which an individual might belong. Families are another such group. Shaped by biological and/or strong social relationships, families provide a web of relationships with tremendous effect on all members, creating a context for health throughout life in the living environment provided and behaviors learned. Whether one currently lives alone or in a family unit, this formative influence continues. Health and illness is not only experienced by individuals, but may influence the whole family as well.

When functioning well, a family can enhance the welfare of all members. Therefore, any church activities that help support the family will have an indirect positive influence on health. For example, Peace Lutheran has designated family Sundays to encourage taking time to intentionally be together without television or video games. The health ministry provides booklets of suggested age-appropriate activities for families. Ministries of health can also target family well-being through offering health education directed at the family unit. Workshops on developing parenting skills, providing support for family caregivers, and companionship during significant life transitions such as birth and death, can all improve family health.

PROMOTING CONGREGATIONAL HEALTH

Just as it is with families, the health of congregations can also be enhanced or diminished by the collective behavior of the group. The experience of worship can enhance health through connection with the transcendent. Preaching biblical themes of health and healing can help articulate for the community why health is of concern to the church. Rituals such as healing services can also communicate a connection between faith and health. From a practical perspective, ensuring a safe and accessible church building will enhance congregational well-being.

The health of the congregation can be promoted through health programs that concentrate on individuals or groups. For example, a health minister may in the role as counselor talk with one member about the importance of exercise for cardiovascular health. This approach may have a positive affect on the individual. However, more people could be reached with a class on cardiovascular health or an intergenerational exercise event such as a family night at the local health club or church Olympics, incorporating a range of skill levels. A health minister might also talk about diet with an individual at risk for developing diabetes. This same issue could be addressed in congregational life by changing the food offered during coffee hour, as we read about St. Stan's doing in chapter 5, or organizing a potluck and exchanging recipes with low fat foods, thus creating a social environment supportive of healthy eating. Simple health education messages provided in a church newsletter or bulletin board can potentially reach large numbers of people as well.

PROMOTING HEALTH THROUGH HEALTH EDUCATION

Education, advocacy, and influencing the behavior of people are all common church activities that can be used to positively influence health in a way that is consistent with the theological beliefs of the congregation. So it should not be a surprise that health education is a significant component of most health ministries. Education can be provided independently or in partnership with other organizations such as the American Heart Association, whose Search Your Heart program specifically targets churches. The numerous health organizations that have recognized the benefits of partnering with churches to reach groups of people can be identified in the National Calendar of Health Observances.[9]

From the church's perspective, making space available for providing community health programs is one way churches promote health through faith-placed health education. In this case the church is a site for health education, but there is no intent to integrate a faith perspective. Many studies have looked at faith-placed health education, most frequently in African American churches, and found the church setting effective for blood pressure screening, weight reduction, and exercise.[10] Providing information is a basic function of congregational life, so providing health information is not a big stretch. For many churches faith-placed health education offers a low-risk, minimum commitment approach to beginning health promotion activities.

Another approach is faith-based health education that actively integrates faith with health education. There are a growing number of educational materials and programs providing resources for faith-based health education. Margie Hesson's books *Health Yourself* and *Stress Less* and Howard Clinebell's

Anchoring Your Well Being are good examples of health education materials that integrate a faith perspective with a wealth of health education information. For some participants, adding the faith perspective will strengthen the motivation for engaging in healthy behaviors. Faith-based health education also has the potential to transform the understanding of health for the congregation as a whole.

In addition to prepared materials, there has been a growing interest on the part of partnering organizations to allow the church to integrate a particular faith perspective in health interventions. While there may be a common public health message to be conveyed to multiple churches, taking the effort to develop a program that can be tailored to the culture of each individual congregation increases the likelihood of success. Heart, Body and Soul in Baltimore, Maryland, was one of the first programs to intentionally integrate faith with a health intervention to reduce cigarette smoking in urban African American churches. Sponsored by Johns Hopkins Medical School, the program actively incorporated church leadership, structure, and values into developing and implementing a program uniquely suited to the culture of the church and led by lay leadership. Educational materials were created in collaboration with the research team and church leaders, incorporating spiritual material, Bible passages, devotional material, sermons, and gospel music. Volunteers were trained to lead the smoking cessation classes.[11]

While in years past health professionals saw churches as convenient locations for community programs, now more health professionals and church members are seeing the importance of integrating church values and beliefs into health programs. Organizations partnering with churches are recognizing that health promotion programs will be more effective if a church can integrate its unique faith perspective, and churches are recognizing that whatever they do in the area of health needs to be theologically sound. Both faith-placed health education and faith-based health education can have a positive influence on the health of communities when used appropriately.

PROMOTING COMMUNITY HEALTH

There is much important work that churches have done and can do to have a positive influence on the health of their congregations, and for a church just beginning, addressing the health of individuals, families, and the congregation as a whole is often the logical place to start. However, the work of health ministry will not be done, and its full potential will not have been reached, until we look outward beyond the church doors. The church is primarily a religious institution, but it is also a community institution, as demonstrated most effectively in the African American community.[12] Its faith message calls people to communities that create health and wholeness and holds potential influence over community health as it exerts its moral authority and provides space, volunteers, and networks of connection to address issues of community concern.

As health ministries like Peace Lutheran's grow, expanding the vision to include not only individuals, but also families, the congregation, and the community, they acknowledge the communal dimension of health consistent with scripture. The Bible is concerned with the well-being of the people of Israel, the nation, and all of creation rather than the health of individuals.[13] Public health offers a framework that many churches would find compatible to this biblical perspective and the concept of community outreach. Directing interventions toward groups or communities and using collective efforts, public health works to assure conditions that enable people to be healthy through promoting health and preventing disease. Because the root issues of health problems are seen in the social, political, occupational, emotional, and physical environments, public health efforts are directed at creating environments where health for all is possible.[14] Policy changes, government regulations, and social marketing are tools for large-scale public health efforts. Group health education and community development are additional tools used in local communities.

As a nation we have a public health plan, Healthy People 2010, created to plot a course for achieving health for all through promoting healthy behaviors, preventing and reducing disease, and promoting healthy and safe communities. Increasing quality and years of healthy life, and eliminating health disparities are its two goals, which would be compatible with the values and beliefs of most churches. Interventions need to be addressed to communities rather than individuals, and many community partnerships will be required to accomplish these goals. Churches can use Healthy People 2010 as guidelines in their health ministries and/or work with other partners to create healthy communities.[15]

Public health professionals have been increasingly interested in the potential of churches to promote healthy communities. Government agencies such as the Center for Disease Control have sought to work with churches on public health issues such as AIDS. Local, state, and federal governments have come to recognize the tremendous potential of churches to improve community health, as reflected in the creation of the White House Office of Faith-Based and Community Initiatives. Whereas previously government would have seen partnering with congregations as a violation of the separation of church and state, there is now a recognition that many community health issues cannot be effectively addressed without bringing churches into the conversation.

Within their own context, churches can focus on the health of populations using a similar framework to public health. Churches can make health promoting policy changes that will enhance the well-being of all members, such as scheduling meetings and events in ways that support Sabbath rest and family time. Churches can also use the principles of social marketing to make positive health behaviors such as healthy eating more acceptable when key leaders set a positive example and health education is offered. The principle of self-direction basic to community development can be used both within the church and in community partnerships. Practically applied, this means that the strengths and resources of any church or community group perceived as having a need the health ministry could address should be engaged in planning and developing appropriate services for themselves.

Transformation for health is a concept related to community development. This popular approach used in the faith and health movement shares the concern of public health to address the root causes of health and disease, and the concern of community development to work from the inside out. Based on the work of Paulo Freire, this approach believes the most powerful impact on community health happens when people come together, analyze the issues, and work to transform society.[16] Acts of justice addressing the root problems of human need can be a challenge for the church, which is often more comfortable with acts of compassion and mercy for needy persons. Yet, improving the health of communities often involves addressing issues of justice in order to transform the experience of health.

Churches not only work with their neighborhood communities, but many also participate in a community of churches through denominations. Joined together by common beliefs, denominations are able to do ministry that would be difficult for an individual church to accomplish—such as missions, health care institutions, retirement communities, and publications. In the past twenty years a growing number of denominations have developed written materials about health ministries, appointed resource people, or organized denominational networks of people involved in health ministries. This development is one reflection of the enthusiasm on the local church level that has the potential to positively influence the health of communities, the nation, and the world.

We have seen the potential of churches to promote the health of individuals, families, congregations, and communities on multiple levels. The church has demonstrated its power to promote health through both intrinsic and intentional health ministries that reach out to those within the congregation and the surrounding community. The church has demonstrated its power to promote health through social outreach ministries and community development efforts to make neighborhoods hospitable and effective, creating environments where health for all is possible. The church has demonstrated its power to promote health through the work of denominations to define and describe health ministries as resources are provided for local churches seeking to continue the healing ministry of Jesus. The church has demonstrated its power to promote health through its health care institutions, free health clinics, and international missions, which have had a positive influence on the health of countless individuals and communities.

Churches can work independently to improve the health of individuals, families, and the congregation as a whole and reach out to their neighborhoods. To fully realize their potential to cultivate healthy communities, churches need to engage in partnerships. The task is too great and complex to be accomplished alone.

QUESTIONS FOR REFLECTION

1. How do people in this congregation understand that their religious participation influences their health?
2. How is health and healing integrated in the life of this congregation?
3. How would you describe this church's involvement with the surrounding community?
4. Both "faith-placed" and "faith-based" health programs can be beneficial to communities. Which approach do you think this church would find most appealing and why?
5. How might the goals of Healthy People 2010 fit with the values and beliefs of this congregation?

IDEAS FOR CONGREGATIONAL ENGAGEMENT

1. Identify the intrinsic health ministry of the church in conversation with members.
2. Find out this church's previous and current involvement in community issues.
3. Review the available resources for faith-based health education and determine suitability for this congregation.

7

FAITH AND HEALTH PARTNERSHIPS

The Potential of Collaboration

When churches work collaboratively with others, more can be done to make their neighborhoods healthy and hospitable than could possibly be accomplished alone. Similarly, when health care organizations partner with the religious community, they create a stronger team to address issues of mutual concern. The determinants of health are complex, and the challenge of improving the health of communities requires partners with different yet compatible perspectives. Diverse individuals and diverse organizations can all contribute to a comprehensive approach. Locally, churches, synagogues, mosques or temples, public health departments, hospitals, social service agencies, and schools are all potential partners sharing a vested interest in healthy communities. Regionally and nationally, government health agencies, voluntary health associations such as the American Heart Association, and philanthropic foundations are also potential partners. When churches work with other organizations building on the unique strengths and assets of each organization to address a shared community health concern, they are able to do something together that could not be done alone.

Partnerships can be as simple as a Health Care Justice Sabbath or as complex as a faith-based primary care clinic. Partnerships with government health agencies are happening on the local, state, and national levels. For example, on the local level, the Frederick County Health Department in Maryland has a Public Health in Parish Nursing program in partnership with local congregations.[1] On the state level, the California Department of Health Services "5 A Day" program is partnering with African American churches to increase the consumption of fresh fruits and vegetables.[2] On the national level the Bureau of Primary Health Care's Faith and Health Partnership builds relationships between federally funded community health centers and faith-based organizations to increase access to health care.[3]

"Over the years, it has become clear that individual health is closely linked to community health. . . . Likewise, community health is profoundly affected by the collective behaviors, attitudes and beliefs of everyone who lives in the community. . . . Partnerships, particularly when they reach out to non-traditional partners, can be among the most effective tools for improving the health of communities."[4]

AN EXAMPLE: CHURCH HEALTH SERVICES

Church Health Services in Beaver Dam, Wisconsin, is the result of one congregation engaging partners to address the issue of access to health care in their community. It began with the vision of one person, Dr. Mike Augustson, who shared a concern with his pastor at Trinity United Methodist Church in 1992 about people without health insurance. This led to developing a task force with representatives from many churches and organizations. From their efforts and with the support of the local hospital and businesses, a free health clinic was created to serve people without private insurance or Medicaid/Medicare. Today, Church Health Services (CHS) is providing comprehensive wholistic care with several paid staff and numerous volunteers.

CHS has engaged a variety of partners to serve its patients including churches, the local hospital, the county health department, schools of nursing and medicine, several private foundations, pharmaceutical companies, and local businesses. Each partner organization contributes what is within its capacity, with the core organization coming from the involved congregations. Together they are able to do something that none of them could do alone for significantly less money than it would cost the local hospital to provide a free health clinic offering the same level of care.

This multifaceted approach to health ministries is unique. The free clinic provides one significant component, and the clinic and parish nurse (CAP) program working with local congregations provides another. Through this program nurses are employed to serve as parish nurses in four churches and work for one clinic a month, providing a connection between the church and clinic.

CHS is influencing not only the health of patients, but the health of the community as well. The majority of the physicians and nurses providing care are volunteers, so they bring their experience of integrating faith and health back to their primary practice sites. CHS has also indirectly influenced community health through the recruitment of physicians, as the opportunity to volunteer at CHS has been a draw for recruiting new physicians to this small community.

Why has CHS been successful in establishing and maintaining partnerships? According to Lois Augustson, executive director, it is because everybody does a little bit and there is an efficient way to engage people and organizations in serving or contributing. There can be a lot of different levels of participation, from volunteering to financial donations to providing in-kind services of labor or equipment. Sharing the burden and responsibility through realistic expectations of each individual, group, or organization is one advantage of partnerships. The manageable size of the Beaver Dam community and its culture of community concern is another reason for its success as well as its historic Christian identity. People perceive themselves as belonging to a church even if they do not attend regularly. Church Health Services works because it fits with the culture of the Beaver Dam community.

LEVELS OF PARTNERSHIP

Partnerships can be simple or complex and may involve working with local, regional, or national organizations. They can

occur on the basic level of communication, through cooperation, coordination, and the most complex levels of collaboration and coalition.[5] The level of partnership a church chooses
will depend on the health issue being addressed and may vary
over time. Communication is the most basic level of partnership. Simply sharing information with other congregations and
organizations, such as distributing flyers for health ministry
activities, both provides a partnership and creates the opportunity to build relationships for future joint ventures. As communication with other groups develops there is the possibility of
working together through cooperation and coordination on different events and programs. A church may choose to cooperate
with the American Heart Association (AHA) Red Dress Sunday
as a way to increase the awareness of women and heart disease. AHA provides the information and coordinates the national event and congregations cooperate to disseminate the information. There is no joint planning between the church and
AHA. Churches simply choose if they want to cooperate with
the resources of this national event.

A church may also coordinate health ministry events with
other organizations. In this case the mission and goals of the
involved organizations need to be compatible. Joint planning is
required for the specific events and there is some sharing of
leadership, control, and risk. A health fair coordinated between
several churches and a local hospital would be one example of
such a partnership.

When churches move to the level of collaboration and participating in coalitions, they find strength in working together
as the combined impact of their resources are maximized. A
new mission and goals are created and either a new organizational structure is formed or a clearly defined division of labor
is established. Longer term projects can be undertaken in this
format.[6] One example is the Institute for Public Health and
Faith Collaboration of the Interfaith Health Program at Emory
University that is bringing together teams from public health
and religious organizations to improve the health of their communities. The collaborative efforts of such coalitions can ad-

dress complex community health problems more effectively than any one organization could do independently.

DYNAMICS OF PARTNERSHIPS

The collaborative nature of partnerships brings people together to work towards a common goal, ultimately creating a shared vision. The characteristics of faith and health partnerships speak to the relational significance of naming and reclaiming the church's role in health. Effective partnerships require strong relationships between organizations and between individuals. Developing strong interpersonal relationships as a foundation for collaboration is created is essential, particularly when bringing together diverse organizations without a common history.

Finding common ground, sharing power, and defining mutual benefits will emerge from the relationships established. The process of collaboration that is essential to partnerships will be influenced by many factors. Members should share a stake in both the process and the outcomes. Multiple layers of participation should be possible. The collaborative process should be characterized by flexibility and adaptability. Clear roles and policies are needed. The work of the partnership should proceed at an appropriate pace that meets the needs of the project without being overwhelming.[7] Building on its inherent strengths within faith and health partnerships, the church brings its social and spiritual capital while public health brings its knowledge of the dynamics of health for individuals and communities.[8]

In the case of partnerships between churches and public health agencies, each has a different primary purpose, yet they both share an interest in the well-being of their community and the disenfranchised. When brought together by a common concern, there is much these partners can learn from each other. Public Health departments may be surprised to learn how much churches already do that positively influences health. Churches may be surprised to learn of shared interests with departments of health. Health care organizations wanting to partner with churches need to understand the dynamics of ministry in general, and the particular dynamics of partnering churches.

Churches partnering with health care organizations need to understand the mission and the purpose of the partnering organization and learn something about health care. Each organization involved in a partnership will bring its own mission, values, and organizational culture to the experience of partnership. Differences must be respected as common ground is established, and programs or services emerging from the partnership need to be culturally acceptable to all involved.[9]

It takes time and effort to develop effective partnerships. They cannot be created overnight. Successful collaboration is able to build on a history of cooperative community efforts, mutual respect, understanding, and trust. Partnerships should represent an appropriate and diverse cross-section of members who hold a shared vision and see collaboration as in their self-interest. Effective partnerships work towards concrete and attainable goals. They are undergirded with sufficient financial, material, and human resources, including skilled leadership. Finally, they are realistic about the time necessary to accomplish their shared vision.[10] These are all qualities reflected in the example of Church Health Services.

In the case of Church Health Services, the partnership began with the vision of one individual working through one church, which then expanded to include a whole community. Frequently faith and health partnerships are initiated by a health organization or academic institution, often because of a mission imperative or external funding. When a grant prompts the formation of partnerships the focus will be time specific. Partnerships may also be formed to address a particular concern, and once the issue is resolved the need for the partnership no longer exists. In other cases partnerships may be ongoing efforts to improve the health and well-being of a neighborhood. For many congregations a partnership provides the training, education, and support to begin a health ministry, as was the case for Peace Lutheran Church, but once it is in place the need for outside partners is diminished. It is a wise organization that develops a realistic plan that can firmly establish a program during the grant period so local congregations will not be left floundering when the grant ends and support from the partnering organization is diminished or withdrawn.

Organizations initiating a partnership may come with a very general agenda, such as a hospital engaging congregations in health ministries for community outreach, or there may be a very specific agenda, such as working with churches to reduce the rate of HIV/AIDS. In either case, the church needs to perceive that collaboration will be beneficial to them. Organizations initiating partnerships should involve potential partners from the very beginning in planning the program. While the majority of faith and health partnerships have been initiated by health organizations or academic institutions, there is no reason why a church with a vision for improving the health of the community could not also be the instigator. This may become more common as churches grow in their understanding of their role in health.

PARTNERS

Hospitals were one of the first partners in congregationally based health ministries to develop parish nursing and health ministry programs, often as part of their community outreach efforts. Public health departments, nursing homes, and home health agencies have also partnered with churches in developing health ministries at one time or another. The first parish nurse programs were started by a hospital, Lutheran General in Park Ridge, Illinois, and an Area Agency on Aging, Northwest Aging Association in Spencer, Iowa, as they partnered with local congregations.

The creation of foundations from the sale of nonprofit hospitals has created another dimension to partnerships. Several have chosen to fulfill their mission by providing direct service to communities through collaborative efforts in faith and health. The Deaconess Foundation in St. Louis supports a number of local parish nurses and the International Parish Nurse Resource Center.[11] The Queens Care Faith and Health Partnership in Los Angeles has a public-private coalition of churches, schools, and social service agencies providing wellness counseling, health education, and health services through parish nurses and community health workers, with the services of Queens Care clinics available for people needing more care.[12]

Public health departments have increasingly been open to collaboration with churches. They have a humanitarian motivation while churches have a religious motivation. Nevertheless, each can find common ground in the pursuit of social justice and the desire to enhance the well-being of individuals, families, and communities. Public health has a mandated responsibility to improve the well-being of communities while churches have a theological imperative to care for the poor, sick, and marginalized in society.[13] Developing partnerships is essential to reaching the goals of Healthy People 2010, and any community assessment would reveal churches as a rich neighborhood resource. Similarly, public health agencies are an important part of the communities where churches exist and potential partners for health ministry collaboration. A range of the areas for collaboration can be found in reviewing the presentations of the American Public Health Association's Caucus on Public Health and the Faith Community. In 2003 an interesting array of research and practice information on faith and health partnerships addressed violence prevention, substance abuse, AIDS, diabetes, exercise, and nutrition. The lead agencies in these partnerships were public health agencies, universities, or national health organizations.[14]

PARTNERSHIP POSSIBILITIES

On the congregational level, identifying resources, assets, and interests in community health issues among members will help prepare the groundwork for partnerships, as will contacting potential partners to discuss community health issues of mutual concern and exploring possible funding sources. At the most basic level, congregations will find many local and national health organizations that are willing to share health information as a way of communicating their message—such as the National Donor Sabbath sponsored by the Department of Health and Human Services.

The American Heart Association was one of the first national health organizations to work with churches, teaching lay people how to check blood pressure. Today their Search Your Heart program also provides information about cardiovascular wellness and training for church leaders to promote healthy lifestyles.[15]

The Witness Project, based at the Arkansas Cancer Research Center, also offers churches information and a program.[16] Using the tradition of giving a witness of one's spiritual journey, breast cancer survivors share their journey with breast cancer, address common fears, and stress the importance of early detection. Lay health advisors teach breast self-exam. Started in African American churches, the program is expanding to include Latina churches as well. This is a good example of developing culturally appropriate health messages.

The complex health issues of HIV/AIDS have highlighted the need for faith and health partnerships locally, nationally, and globally. Balm in Gilead is a not-for-profit international organization working with the faith community to prevent the spread of HIV/AIDS throughout the African Diaspora.[17] It has developed culturally appropriate health educational materials for African American churches and provides training, organizational, and technical assistance to churches and health departments working with churches.

Philanthropic organizations such as the Robert Wood Johnson Foundation encourage faith and health partnerships through funding new initiatives. Their funding began one of the first volunteer parish nurse program in northwest Iowa through a partnership between congregations and an area agency on aging. Currently their Faith in Action program funds interfaith volunteer caregivers to support persons in the community with long-term health needs. Many other foundations, such as the Retirement Research Foundation, Wheat Ridge Ministries, and the Rapides Foundation, to name a few, have provided funding for new health ministry initiatives.

Whatever their configuration, faith and health partnerships multiply the human and material resources available to address community health problems. Partnerships such as Church Health Services, on an organizational level, reflect the interdisciplinary nature of health ministries found on the congregational level. In the same way that congregationally based health ministries are enhanced by diverse perspectives from various health professionals, clergy, and interested lay people, community health initiatives are enhanced when diverse organizations with a common concern join in partnership to transform the health of communities. It is tempting for congregations to want to be lone rangers in ministries of health, focusing only on their concerns and using only their resources. While it may be easier to work alone, the journey towards community wellness requires many workers.

There are many possibilities for partnerships for churches wanting to have a positive influence on the health of their communities. Partnerships can provide an opportunity to develop or expand congregationally based health ministries. As the possibilities are considered, it is important to realize that culture, values, and local context will influence what is appropriate for each congregation. Some congregations have a long history of collaborative ventures. Other congregations have always worked independently. Neighborhoods will vary as well in their foundation for potential partnerships. Creating a vision for collaboration requires understanding the potential benefits to the congregation and the community. Whether or not it is appropriate for your congregation at this point in time, any congregation whose health ministry develops into maturity is likely to participate in one or more partnerships. Collaboration will be imperative if the church desires to positively influence neighborhood health. As ministries of health uniquely suited to your local context are created, there are many different models to consider whatever the church's vision for promoting health, healing, and wholeness.

QUESTIONS FOR REFLECTION

1. What, if any, has been this congregation's prior experience with partnerships?

2. Would this congregation be interested in identifying partners for health ministries? What might be significant issues in developing faith and health partnerships?

3. What community health issues, if any, have been effectively addressed in your area through partnerships between congregations and the public health/community health agencies?

4. What would your community look like if it were really a healthy place to live? What would need to change? What existing strengths could be used to make it healthier?

IDEAS FOR CONGREGATIONAL ENGAGEMENT

1. Talk with your local health department or hospitals to find out what they do, or might be interested in doing, with congregations.

2. Talk with other congregations to explore the possibilities for partnering in ministries of health. If there is a local clergy association this may be a good group with which to speak.

3. Check out the Interfaith Health Program website www.ihpnet.org to read materials on faith and health partnerships. Share this material with the health ministry team.

8

MODELS OF HEALTH MINISTRY

An invitation to participate in a faith and health partnership is one way a church may first consider how it might intentionally promote health. Sometimes an individual who feels called to a health ministry is the instigating factor. Other times, familiarity with current models of health ministry invites a church to explore the possibilities. Health ministries are one of many ways a congregation may choose to care for each other. Whether the church membership is small, medium, or large; whether it is located in the country, suburbs, or city; whether there are few or abundant financial and human resources; any church can have a positive influence on health. Once a church has made a decision to intentionally promote health, there are many possible approaches from which to choose or new paradigms can be created uniquely suited to the culture and local context of your congregation.

As we consider some of the models of health ministry, remember that models are just that. They are not the ministry; rather, they provide a structure that facilitates health ministries. The members of the church need to give life and breath to the structures to transform them into an authentic ministry.

We have seen several models of health ministry in the examples considered in the preceding chapters. Redwood Covenant has a nurse serving as the director of health ministry as an unpaid staff person. St. Stan's has a health ministry cabinet, including several parish nurses and other health professionals. Having established a strong health ministry, they are now considering hiring a parish nurse. Peace Lutheran began with a health ministry cabinet, then added the staff position of health advocate. Currently, they are looking to hire a parish nurse. Church Health Services provides direct clinical care, relying heavily on volunteers. They have employed nurses in a combined role of serving as parish nurses and also working in the clinic to strengthen the connection between the churches and CHS. Queens Care, mentioned in chapter 7, employs parish nurses and community health workers working together.

The possibilities of what health ministries might look like are as numerous as the congregations who might consider such a ministry. Here are some of the prevalent models to consider in developing intentional health ministries. A health cabinet or health ministry team may provide the organizing framework. Health ministries may be developed around key leadership roles such as a parish nurse, health minister, or lay health promoter. Some churches may choose to provide direct health services through a faith-based health clinic. Programs of care may shape or contribute to a health ministry. Some churches choose to respond to the social and political dynamics of health through advocacy and health initiatives. None of these approaches are mutually exclusive or permanent. As a health ministry grows and matures there may be a need for new and different models.

HEALTH CABINET

It is tempting when a church wants to intentionally promote health to jump into doing programs or thinking someone needs to be hired to "do" health ministry. Yet it is imperative that critical groundwork be laid first for health ministries to be sustainable, as will be discussed in chapter 9. Whether a health cabinet is the organizational structure for providing health ministries or offers support for another model, forming a group to support health ministries is critical.

The health cabinet brings together people passionate about health to be catalysts for health ministry, who may or may not be health professionals. As an umbrella group concerned about health, the health cabinet will have three primary approaches to integrating health in the life of the church. One is to identify what happens in the church that is healthy and unhealthy. Another is to encourage other church groups to integrate health into their ministries. The final approach is to provide health programs.[1] "I would say that even if the health cabinet never produced a program, suggested a health regimen, or probed into a related biblical-theological position concerning healing, it has done its job if it has helped in the permeation of an attitude of the church as a place of health and care and empathy and exchange of human love."[2]

A health cabinet provides the opportunity for wider involvement of the church community and also increases the likelihood that the health ministries developed will be relevant to the congregation, and not just the idea of one person. When the cabinet is also responsible for implementing health ministries they may plan health education events, gather folks together to work on health advocacy, develop support groups, plan healing services, and organize informal care giving. For many churches a health cabinet may be the best fit for their personal and financial resources as they begin health ministries. Other churches may want to consider staff positions that can help actualize health ministries. Three key leadership roles have emerged to help the church promote health: parish nurse, health minister, and lay health promoter.

PARISH NURSE

Parish nursing is one of the best known models of health ministry. While a parish nurse may also be considered a health minister, a health minister is not necessarily a parish nurse. *Whether or not you are a nurse,* it is important for anyone interested in health ministries to be familiar with this model because the development of the field has been strongly influenced by parish nurses.

A parish nurse is a registered nurse with additional training in this role. There is no way to know how many nurses are practicing as parish nurses. Many serve in this capacity as unpaid staff, and many who are in paid positions are working part time. We do know that about 10,000 people have completed a course using the International Parish Nurse Resource Center's parish nurse curriculum.[3] In the health ministry program I previously led, working with nurses volunteering in their own congregations, the nurses had regular times when they were available for one-to-one contacts when people could ask questions about their health or have their blood pressure checked. They planned and/or led health education programs, provided health education through bulletin inserts and bulletin boards or health fairs, and offered health screenings. Some of the nurses visited people who were homebound or started support groups for grief, weight loss, or persons caring for the elderly or infirm. They served as advocates and were available to help people find resources they needed for health care and social services.[4]

Parish nursing was recognized as a specialty by the American Nurses Association in 1998, and as such now has its own scope and standards of practice.[5] Parish nursing has concerns particular to the profession, yet there is much that can be applied to health ministries in general by considering this specialty area. There is much to be learned from many different disciplines as we engage in ministries of health.

The purpose of health ministry is not to re-create what is already available in the health care system, but to provide services not readily available in a manner that consistently integrates faith and health. Reflecting some of the gaps in our health care system, parish nurses function independently in the roles of educator, counselor, referral agent, advocate, facilitator, and integrator of faith and health.[6] Health ministers also function in these roles within the parameters of their own professional background. Similarly, lay health promoters may participate in providing related services under supervision and within the scope of their training and competency. In addition, when a health cabinet is coordinating health ministries, it may make provision for the services represented in these roles to be provided.

Recognizing that one's professional background will influence how one serves in these roles, the term health minister will be used in the following discussion of roles as the more inclusive term.

Health Educator

Health education can be simultaneously the easiest and the most difficult task. It is easy in the sense that there are many groups, both hospitals and disease specific associations, which are more than glad to come and provide health education in a church. There are also excellent books created for study groups that integrate faith and health (Appendix B). Health education is difficult because it takes a great deal of thought, effort, and planning to make health education a meaningful learning experience and not just an event or activity. It also takes more effort to make health education faith-based, when issues of faith are intertwined with the health content, as opposed to faith-placed, when the church building provides the location for health education. Any effective health education begins with identifying congregational concerns for which health education could provide some answers. This is why understanding congregational culture has been emphasized as an integral part of developing effective health ministries.

Health education may occur in groups or with individuals. It can also be provided through articles in the church bulletin or newsletter or through bulletin boards.[7] In my previous health ministry program, we created bulletin board materials for all of the congregations to use, providing basic health information and always finding a scriptural context for the material. Information on other health educational opportunities in the community can also be provided to the congregation. Being familiar with credible Internet websites for health information, such as the government sponsored sites of the National Institutes of Health,[8] can contribute to health education, as can helping people discern reliable health information. Since there is no quality control on who makes information accessible online, it is important to help people identify the source of information and be sure that it is from a reputable organization or individual.[9] One congregation with which I worked had nurses available one evening a week when folks could use the church computers to look up health information and the nurse could help them discern the reliability of the information.

Health Counselor

Providing guidance to parishioners regarding health concerns can be a valuable part of health ministries. This type of activity often happens informally in many churches as members seek out health professionals for advice. In my own experience providing a nurse drop-in center at a church, I found that health counseling frequently involved an individual trying to ascertain if he or she should see a physician, and if so, how to approach the visit. Other common topics were utilizing the health care system, family concerns, care giving, and complementary medicine.

Health counseling may occur informally in the halls of the church or on the street, or it may occur in regularly scheduled office hours. The goal is to help empower the individual to deal with his or her health concern in an effective manner. By taking the time to listen and reflect constructively, the health counselor may help the individual discover his or her own wisdom and resources.

In counseling, as with health education, it is essential to work within your professional knowledge and refer matters beyond your expertise. Always be mindful of your limitations as well as your abilities in this role. Maintaining privacy and confidentiality is essential to the role of health counselor. Health professionals also need to be familiar with their practice acts that may require reporting on matters such as abuse that may be revealed in a health counseling situation.

Referral Agent and Advocate

The roles of referral agent and advocate are closely interrelated. The complexity of our health care system can challenge anyone, so helping people find appropriate health and social services can be a valuable part of health ministry. Some churches, such as Peace Lutheran, may even make the role of health advocate a staff position. Familiarity with both community and church resources is necessary to be an effective advocate and provide appropriate referrals. Visiting the clinics or social service agencies to which you are most likely to refer is a good way to get a sense of the kind of services provided, as is developing relationships with each staff. Sharing information about referral sources in the community among church personnel can be a good way of sharing resources and identifying gaps in services. Once a referral has been given, be sure to have the person referred report back so you know if that individual received the help needed.

It is also important to realize there may be many referral sources within your own church. For example, you may wish to refer someone to the prayer chain, a group that would provide meals on a short term basis, or to Stephen's Ministers, who might provide some lay visitation. Knowing what is available within your church is as important as knowing what is available in your community.

Functioning as an advocate means first being clear about what people want as you help them discern the nature of their key issues. One's knowledge of health and the health care system can then be used to empower them to get what they need. Listening, interpreting, guiding, empowering, and accompanying may all be part of advocacy.

Facilitator

No health minister or health cabinet can provide all the care a church might need. A facilitator can work with support groups that may be created to provide an opportunity for people with a common concern such as grief or a shared health concern such as diabetes to learn from each other. The ability of others to provide care through volunteering can also be facilitated. Working with volunteers provides an opportunity to expand the ministry, as well as providing opportunities for people to serve their church. I once heard a presentation at a parish nurse conference titled "Even Jesus Had Twelve Disciples." This program used a team approach that divided responsibilities among a group where one person might be responsible for coordination, one person worked with the elderly and persons who were homebound, and one person worked to have health education literature available in brochures, posters, and news items.[10] Each person could contribute something within his or her capabilities and the burden could be shared. The other creative thing about this presentation was the connection its title made between health ministry and the gospels. The obvious reminder that Jesus had a team working with him can be a good reminder to today's health ministers.

Integrator of Faith and Health

Effective health ministries weave faith and health throughout everything that is done. This may be reflected explicitly in conversations, presentations, or prayer, or incorporated into worship. It may be implicit in the fact that health is being addressed in a congregational setting or reflected in the life of the health minister. This is not to say that a health minister needs to be a perfect reflection of the interrelationships between faith and health, only that the he or she should be growing in this area. The ability of the health minister to lead the congregation in integrating faith and health is dependent on his or her own faith journey. Finding support with others involved locally in health ministries can provide insight for integrating faith and health. Attending national conferences such as the Health Ministries Association or the Westberg Symposium for parish nurses can give health ministers additional support. Some health ministers choose to pursue theological education to grow in their understanding of the integration of faith and health.

UNIQUE ASPECTS OF RECEIVING CARE IN A CHURCH

One of the questions that ultimately needs to be considered in developing any model of health ministries is what distinguishes services provided in the church setting from the traditional health care system. I explored this topic in two studies. The first looked at clients' perceptions of receiving nursing care in two Catholic parishes.[11] We found that the atmosphere of the church, the convenience of this setting, the time available for interaction, and practically experiencing the connection between faith and health distinguished the church experience from traditional health care settings. The emotional dimension of the nurse-client interaction was as important to the participants as any nursing service they received, and people described a variety of ways they felt cared for by the nurse. We surmised that the nurse's reliance on interpersonal rather than technical interventions in a congregational setting enhanced the caring experience.

The second study looked at a group of volunteer parish nurses and their perspectives on what they experienced as unique in providing care in a church setting.[12] The nurses felt they had the greatest impact through health promotion/prevention, advocacy, health education, and health counseling, including psychosocial support and spiritual care. The nurses appreciated the unique opportunities afforded by the congregational setting including integrating faith and health in nursing practice, the more relaxed environment, the opportunity for long-term relationships, and the level of professional autonomy. Challenges were experienced in the areas of client autonomy, the impact of religious beliefs, and the nurse's worship experience and time constraints.

In both studies the role of the nurse as an advocate stood out as being particularly important. Clients described, "It's like a stepping stone in going to the right place," and "She can give you some pointers in the right direction."[13] Nurses described, "I'm a nonthreatening link to the health care system," and "I go to bat for people."[14] This is significant because advocacy seems to be a role that many people need, and it is significant because it reflects the dominant philosophy that health ministries are provided not to replace existing health services but to help others better access what is available. Advocacy for individuals and for communities has the potential to be transformative.

HEALTH MINISTER

The position of health minister is another way to staff health ministries and also fulfill the roles of educator, counselor, referral agent, advocate, facilitator, and integrator of faith and health. A health minister is someone with experience in health and wellness who is responsible for working with a congregation to promote health. This might be a nurse, social worker, physical therapist, occupational therapist, nutritionist, health educator, or LPN. In the Chicago area one of the early health ministers was a physical therapist.[15] The professional background of the health minister and the needs of the church will shape how this position is developed. When coordinating a volunteer health ministry program, one of my most effective churches was led by an LPN and an AIDS activist who had a passion for health ministry. They engaged a group of individuals with a wide range of professional backgrounds to work in health ministry. Our program originally started only working with nurses but found there were many churches interested in promoting health that did not have a registered nurse willing and able to volunteer, so we expanded to include the role of health minister.

Some nurses will choose to use the term health minister or minister of health instead of parish nurse. This may more closely identify the position with other ministerial staff and identifies in the title that health is a ministry. Whatever words are used to describe the position, they need to be consistent with the church's patterns of language.

LAY HEALTH PROMOTERS/COMMUNITY HEALTH ADVISORS

Lay people trained to address specific health concerns are an important part of health ministries. This role has many names including lay health promoters, lay health advisors, and community health workers. The concept is influenced by international health work that has traditionally used community health workers to make health information more accessible to communities with few if any health professionals. This idea has been particularly popular in the southeastern United States. Often the role of the lay health promoter is to target a specific health concern such as reducing cardiovascular disease.[16] Typically this role is used to access hard-to-reach populations. The workers are members of the target group and their expertise is in the community rather than formal education.[17] Lay people have also been used as advocates to help people better utilize health care resources.[18] The advantage of this role is its ability to reach people who because of language, culture, or resources would not be likely to access traditional health resources. Working with health professionals, lay health promoters can extend the impact of education and advocacy.

DIRECT HEALTH SERVICES

A few congregations will feel called to shape their health ministries around the provision of primary care when access to health care is an issue in their community. This is more costly and labor intensive than other congregationally based health ministries, but can have a significant impact on community health. Few if any churches have adequate resources to develop a faith-based health clinic independently. This model of necessity requires collaboration with other churches and community organizations as we saw in the example of Church Health Services in Beaver Dam, Wisconsin.[19] Churches interested in developing a clinic can draw upon the resources of the Christian Community Health Fellowship to learn about best practices in faith-based clinics.[20]

CARING CONGREGATIONS

Enhancing the ability of congregations to care for each other will have a positive influence on health. The Church of the Brethren built their model for health ministry, "Lafiya," around caring congregations, building on the experience of missionaries in Nigeria who successfully worked with community health workers to provide basic health education. "Lafiya is a word in the Hausa language that means 'well-being,' or 'wholeness.' It can also mean 'How are you?'('Lafiya?') as well as 'I am well.' ('Lafiya!')."[21] Using care groups to listen, empower, and access resources, the program seeks to help people take responsibility for their own health. The image of a tree is used to represent the Lafiya ministry that is rooted in empowering, listening, and "resourcing" and branches out to include both healing ministries and health promotion. This approach builds on the intrinsic health promoting capacity of the church when people experience caring connections.

Lay ministry programs are another approach to caring congregations that can be an important component of health ministries. Recognizing the community responsibility in providing pastoral care, programs such as Stephen's Ministry,[22] or Befriender's Ministry,[23] train lay people to do visitation in people's homes, hospitals, and nursing homes. While the program's intention is relational, frequently health issues are what put persons in the position of needing visitation, and providing these relationships has the potential to enhance the health of both the person being visited and the lay minister.

ADVOCACY/HEALTH INITIATIVES

Congregations concerned about social justice may wish to focus on broader community health issues through political advocacy, focusing on such issues as seeking justice in health care.[24] One congregation with which I worked had an outreach committee that addressed many justice issues such as world hunger, environmental health, and domestic violence, all significant public health issues. A church's health ministry might also emerge around particular health issues that are of concern to their community, such as HIV/AIDS or access to health care.

HEALING MINISTRIES

Many people equate health ministry with the healing ministry of the church, which can be a good place to begin and an essential model to continue. Being intentional about integrating themes of health, healing, and wholeness in worship and liturgy is health promoting, as is using rituals appropriate to your religious tradition, such as healing services and anointing with oil.[25]

HEALTHY CHURCH WORK ENVIRONMENT

In considering health ministries, the church's responsibility to provide a life-affirming work environment for the staff should not be forgotten. Self-care can be a significant issue for clergy because of the demands of their work. Any effective health ministry should be mindful of providing a healthy work environment for church staff as well as the congregation.

PAID OR UNPAID

Whatever model of health ministries a church chooses or creates, there is a place for paid staff and unpaid staff. There are many people volunteering as health ministers who desire to serve their church and are doing very good things. When you look at health ministries from the perspective of the church, there may be good reasons to rely on volunteers, as is true for many of the church's ministries. Depending on available resources, some churches may find volunteers to be the only option to provide health ministries. If a volunteer model is being used, working with a team can help keep the load reasonable and increase the potential impact.

Yet there is a limit to how much time volunteers will have for health ministries. The greater the influence the church hopes to achieve through health ministries, the greater the need for paid staff. We cannot expect volunteers to put in all of the time necessary to significantly improve the health of communities. If a church or partnering organization has a goal of improving the health of the community, then consideration needs to be given to paid parish nurses, health ministers, or lay health promoters. People who are employed in a role will have more time to devote to the task at hand, and improving the health of communities is a considerable task. On the other hand, the church also needs to be careful when choosing a paid model not to assume that a health ministry has been created just by employing a health minister.

Ideally the model chosen should be the best able to accomplish the goals the church has for health ministries with the available resources. Whatever approach is chosen for implementing health ministries, remember that models are tools. They are not the ministry itself, but help to structure how the ministry will be provided. Be willing to think outside of the box. If there doesn't seem to be an appropriate model for your local context, then create your own structure that would facilitate health, healing, and wholeness for your congregation. Being interested in a particular model may prompt a church to consider developing health ministries; however, a firm foundation for integrating health in the life of the church needs to be established before implementing health ministries. Whatever model a church chooses, it takes a whole congregation to make a health ministry effective.

QUESTIONS FOR REFLECTION

1. What existing models of health ministry do you think would be most appropriate for your congregation and why?

2. Do you have a vision for a new model of health ministry that is needed in your church? What would it be?

3. How are other churches in your community doing health ministries?

4. What are the financial resources to support health ministries? (This may influence what model is chosen.)

IDEAS FOR CONGREGATIONAL ENGAGEMENT

1. Consider, along with church leadership, the general model for ministry and how this might be applied to health ministries.

2. Invite people from other churches with different models of health ministry to share their experience with your church.

3. If parish nursing is a model being considered, read *Scope and Standards of Parish Nursing Practice.*

9

CREATING SUSTAINABLE HEALTH MINISTRIES

From the time a decision is made to explore intentional health ministries, a solid foundation needs to be created to ensure sustainability, whatever model of care a congregation chooses. Laying the groundwork of understanding and support will enhance the ministry's effectiveness and increase the likelihood of the ministry continuing if key individuals leave or funding changes. It is not uncommon for churches to have episodic ministries dependent on current interests or available human and financial resources. However, for health ministry to reach its full potential to transform the lives of individuals, families, and communities, it needs to be woven into the life of the church in such a way that health is seen as a natural and necessary dimension of the church's ministry.

There is a common tendency when beginning to quickly provide programs, and there are many valuable health programs a church might offer. Yet if the ground is not adequately prepared then the seeds planted will be short lived and health ministry will only be a program. Just as soil needs to be prepared before the benefits of a garden can be received, a congregation also needs to be prepared to consider health an integral part of their communal life. Tending the foundation for sustainability is an ongoing process that begins as the vision and plans initially develop and continues as long as the ministry is in effect.

Peace Lutheran Church, discussed in chapter 6, is a good example of laying a firm foundation. With the guidance of their sponsoring hospital, they spent a year developing their vision and mission for heath ministries which they defined as "We serve people who have spiritual, physical, emotional, and relational needs with prayer and Christ-centered care." They further defined their ministry goals as "To establish a health ministry at Peace Lutheran Church utilizing a Health Cabinet Model. . . . It is our purpose to facilitate both members of the congregation and the broader community in accessing health care information and services in a compassionate Christian environment." While these are simple statements, they reflect much thought, research, and discussion, and articulate for the congregation why and how health concerns fit into the life of the church. Sustainability is strengthened when health ministries are consistent with the overall mission and vision of the church as understood by members.

CREATING THE VISION

Health ministries need to be created in community and for the community. While there may be critical individuals in leadership positions, a process of communal discernment is needed and the wisdom and desires of the church as a community must be honored. In short, the congregation needs to be engaged in the process of recognizing the many ways church life already influences health and planning for how health can be intentionally promoted as a shared vision for ministries of health emerges. The groundwork begins with understanding the unique congregational culture. If the church is formal and has an organized structure there may be committees to go through and procedures to follow to start a new ministry. If the church is more informal and relational, it may be more important to have the support of key individuals. If you have worked through the reflection questions and ideas for congregational engagement in the previous chapters you will be well on the way to preparing the foundation.

Laying the groundwork for sustainable health ministries begins with several key steps.[1] If the following suggestions for getting started do not fit with the culture of your congregation, consider what would be appropriate for cultivating interest and ownership for health ministries in your church. First bring together members interested in faith and health as a task force, being as creative as possible about who those people might be. If your church has many health professionals, those are one obvious group to include, but you also need committed lay people who are passionate about health. Whether or not the pastor is part of the initial task force, his or her support will be critical. How the pastor understands health and healing will influence the ministry, as will what the pastor says, does, and preaches. Once this group is gathered together, think about what voices from the congregation may be missing. Health ministries will be strengthened to the extent that it is possible to have a group representing the age, gender, and ethnic diversity of the congregation.

As the task force explores who their congregation is and how things are done, they can also consider how health might best be integrated into congregational life, giving it the potential to flourish rather than be a short-lived fad. Key factors in creating health ministries may be revealed by looking at other new areas of ministry that have been established successfully. For example, if this church recently started a thriving prison ministry, while the content is different, by considering their experience you may learn key factors to ministry success particular to your church. The work of the task force should be grounded in the church's religious traditions, seeking God's guidance throughout the process.

Next, as a group you will want to learn all you can about health ministries through reading, visiting websites, and talking with people involved in health ministries. There are many great resources (Appendix B) that can inform your work together. As you read and learn be mindful of the dynamics and theology of your own congregation to determine what material would be compatible with your church.

Once the task force has a sense of the health ministry possibilities, identify what your church is already doing that influences the health of church members and staff. Strong and effective health ministries involve collaboration and teamwork that integrate health in a variety of church activities.[2] A broad understanding of what contributes to health will enable task force members to identify activities intentionally addressing health issues as well as the intrinsic health ministry of the church. This process can be very encouraging and make the possibility of an intentional health ministry more inviting to both the task force and the congregation. Promoting health can seem daunting if presented as a totally new venture, but when the church's present influence on health is recognized, intentional health ministries then become a way of expanding and building on what is already there rather than starting from scratch. From this learning process a vision should begin to emerge of what health ministry might be in your church.

When the task force has an understanding of health ministries, the congregation can then be engaged in exploring how health is currently part of congregational life and the possibilities for what could be in the future. Existing patterns of communication, such as worship, preaching, and adult education, can be used or new opportunities created, such as a forum on the church's challenge in health. A litany of health and healing, reflecting the intrinsic health ministry of the church that can be adapted to your congregation, is offered in Appendix C.[3] An adult education program using a faith-based health education program is another venue that could be used to discuss faith and health.

Ownership of health ministries will increase as the circle of people grows who can articulate how health is a meaningful part of church life. A communal vision of how this place and this people can enhance well-being will be stronger than the dream of one individual or a small group. As the congregation becomes familiar with the idea, begin assessing resources and interests for health ministry within your congregation and community using the suggestions in chapter 5, remembering that this will take a while. An oral or written survey is one tool to learn more about your congregation's interests and resources.

Having taken time to explore the possibilities and gather baseline information, the task force can now consider the model of health ministry best suited to your congregation. The vision and goals for health ministries as well as the available human and financial resources will influence your choices. The task force may grow into a health cabinet that plans and develops programs; you may choose to hire someone in a health ministry staff position; or you may have a volunteer who can assume this role. The tradition of the church in relying on volunteers or paid staff may indicate what would be appropriate staffing for health ministries. Some churches, such as St. Stan's discussed in chapter 5, choose to begin with a volunteer program and then later consider hiring a health ministry staff person after sufficient congregational support is generated. Starting with one model of care does not preclude adding or changing different components over time. Whatever approach is most appropriate to your congregation, the key factor is including a broad base of support so health becomes part of the fabric and values of the congregation.

The words chosen to name the health ministry can have an effect on congregational support. It will impact how a new ministry is perceived, who should participate in its leadership, and who should receive its services. For example, I always recommend exploring the concept of health ministry before focusing on a particular model of health ministry. Parish nursing is an excellent and very effective health ministry role. However, if the conversation begins by talking about parish nursing rather than how the church might develop a ministry of health, people may think nurses are the only people who can be involved.

Whether your health ministry is built around volunteers or staff, there will be costs, so a realistic budget is needed. Some of the practical things to think about in a health ministry budget are supplies such as a blood pressure cuff and stethoscope, educational materials, promotional materials, and refreshments for health events. There may be costs associated with training, professional liability insurance, and travel. The church may want to send people to the Health Ministries Association annual conference or the Westberg Symposium for parish nursing. Budget can be a controversial issue, yet ministries that last in church life usually have solid financial and personnel support. Including health ministries in the church budget is one tangible way of increasing visibility and is also a reflection of making health a priority. Budgeting responsibly is one expression of conscientious stewardship.

Having prepared, planned, and envisioned, the task force's final step in the initial process is to identify and implement several realistic goals and objectives for the proposed health ministry. A reasonable time frame needs to be allowed, taking into account the unique time parameters of church life. Nothing breeds success like success. Remember that goals for health ministry will change over time. A beginning health ministry should start with modest goals; as the ministry matures and people grow in leadership more ambitious goals can be considered.

Articulating objectives and how to measure their achievement is an important part of developing health ministries. Sometimes it is tempting just to get started, but there may be a problem in a year or so without clearly identified objectives and a plan for evaluation when someone asks, "Why should we do this?" Depending on what the church is trying to do, the objectives and evaluation plan may be very simple, but they are necessary. Objectives may be very specific and related to particular target groups or issues. Typically, objectives should be something that can be measured. There should be a way to know that the objective has been achieved. It can be helpful to have a time frame for achieving the objective as well. For example:

- Organize a health ministry cabinet by June.
- Provide a forum on the church and healing during our winter seminar.
- Develop a vision for our health ministry and share it with the congregation by September.

Developing the habit of being clear about the purpose and objectives for health ministries can help in several ways. First, it will help when the congregation needs a written or verbal report about what has happened in health ministries. Second, having a clear vision and measurable objectives will facilitate creating funding proposals either for the church or for an external funder if an opportunity should present itself. Finally, having a clear sense of purpose and defined objectives will help prioritize where time, money, and effort should be expended, including how to respond to new opportunities. If there is no vision for where health ministries are headed, it will be impossible to tell when the destination has been reached.

ORGANIZATIONAL FRAMEWORK

Whatever model of care is chosen, a health cabinet that becomes part of the permanent organizational structure is without a doubt the most significant infrastructure needed to support health ministries. This important group of people, which may or may not be the same as the initial task force, can champion health ministries. Regardless of whether paid or volunteer staff provide leadership, health ministry needs to be formed in and for the community. A health cabinet increases the likelihood that health will become an integral part of congregational life by providing voice, vision, and direction. It gives health a place to hang its hat and people with whom to share the journey.

Connecting and communicating are essential to creating sustainable health ministries. Connecting with key groups within the church as health ministries grow and develop can both strengthen the ministry in the present and contribute to sustainability. Visitation and outreach are two common ministry areas that would likely share some common concerns about health. In addition to modes of internal connection, those involved in health ministry leadership will benefit from connecting with others engaged in similar ministries. This may be done through a local health ministry network, a chapter of the Health Ministries Association, or a denominational health ministry support group. Those involved in health ministries have valued the opportunity to network with persons involved in similar work. In a new area of ministry, the opportunity to learn from others is helpful.[4]

Connecting facilitates opportunities for communication. Communication that both informs the congregation and provides opportunities for their input is critical. Some possible forms of communication include the church newsletter or bulletin, e-mail, web page, sharing oral or written reports, attending other committee meetings, making announcements in church, and telling stories. Churches are places that tell stories, and when a personal face can be put on what happens through health ministries it can go a long way to generate support. In one church with which I worked as a program coordinator, the parish nurse had a dramatic experience of intervening to get needed care for an individual having heart problems during a church service. The remembering and telling of that story transformed how people saw her role in the church.[5]

Worship is a fundamental source of communication. It is what ties the life of the church together, so for ministries of health to flourish themes of health and healing need to periodically be incorporated in the worship life of the church, through the music that is sung, the sermons that are preached, and the rituals that are observed. Worship can be an appropriate way to affirm those serving in health ministries through a commissioning service or other appropriate ritual that marks the official beginning of their service.

EVALUATION

While some of the particulars will vary depending on the health ministry model, evaluation is an important concept to consider from the early stages. Those in church and health ministry leadership need to know whether the desired impact has been achieved. Feedback is needed to know how health ministries can improve. Evaluation is also an important part of stewardship of the church's resources with an associated responsibility to know that the resources going into ministries of health are having a positive influence.[6]

Even in the beginning stages, thought needs to be given to how the success of health ministries will be determined and how the church will decide this is a ministry it wants to continue to support. Program evaluation may sound like a strange concept in association with a church, depending on whether the church is informal or has a more formal, organized structure. Whether or not the word evaluation is ever used in your church, it does happen.[7] It may be the informal evaluation of personal opinion as seen in the story previously mentioned. It may show up in how people are willing to volunteer their time, what programs people are willing to fund, and what programs people are willing to cut.

To be most effective evaluation needs to be built into the process and programs of health ministry from the beginning. Criteria for success need to be determined. Are you willing to have a meaningful short-term ministry or do you want to develop a health ministry that will become a permanent part of church life? Many ministries in church life are time limited and make good contributions while they are in effect.

The ability to evaluate will depend on the foundation laid. The congregation's health ministries can not be evaluated unless there is clarity about what is being done, why it is being done, and what is hoped to be achieved. The basis of the foundation begins with a vision for health ministry that is congruent with the congregation. A vision expresses a broad perspective on what health ministry should be within this church. From there should flow the objectives for the health ministry, and the evaluation should proceed from the objectives. Before there can be clarity about the vision for health ministries, there needs to be clarity about the overall vision for the church.

Some congregations with a very organized structure may also have a procedure for evaluating programs and staff. Many of the organizations that a church might partner with, such as hospitals, departments of health, and educational institutions, require program evaluation. The kind of information that health care organizations or foundations may need will be very different than what would be of interest to most churches. Typical evaluations do not capture the transformation that can take place through the integration of faith and health. Outcome engineering is one approach to program evaluation that has become popular for its ability to take the qualitative stories that are so much a part of the positive impact of health ministries and utilize a formula that converts to a quantitative scale.[8] Telling stories is something that churches understand and frequently do in their own informal evaluation.

A very practical and useful resource for evaluation is available online through the Wheat Ridge Foundation, which has a mission of supporting the ministries of Lutheran churches. Their "Health Ministry Self Study for Congregations" identifies eight indicators that can be used in planning and evaluating health ministries, including the congregation's expression of concern for faith and wellness, support by church leaders, policies to support health ministry, regular health ministry audits that assess needs and perceptions, clearly identified health ministry goals and objectives, sponsoring health ministry programs, using available health and wellness resources, and involvement in the community.[9] The self-study guide is intended for congregations who currently have a health ministry. However, looking at the guide can provide ideas of what to consider in program development that may be helpful in preparing for evaluation.

ACCOUNTABILITY

Sustainable health ministries, however they are implemented, take accountability seriously. While they may be initiated by an individual with a personal sense of call, they recognize that the movement of God's spirit needs to be undergirded with a strong sense of responsibility. Health ministries are not done in isolation, but in community, and therefore involve accountability to others. An awareness of communal and professional accountability is essential to the integrity of sustainable ministry. Responsible behavior, appropriate documentation, and communication are all essential to develop ongoing support for health ministries.[10] Accountability can also be demonstrated through the health minister's behavior, through being responsive to congregational needs and concerns as well maintaining high standards for health ministries.

Each congregation has certain standards for how they do ministry, as well as standards for communication. Depending on the congregation's governance structure, health ministries may be accountable to a church board or committee that shares a broader goal consistent with health ministry. Church leaders are accountable to the congregation for being sure people are appropriately serving within their training, and ensuring that the program is beneficial to the congregation.

Anyone serving in a health ministry role is accountable to the congregation for the quality of the care provided. Persons serving in a volunteer health ministry role will have a different time commitment than those in a paid role, but their accountability remains similar. You are accountable to the people who utilize health ministries to do so in a competent and compassionate manner. Any personal information exchanged needs to remain confidential. Any health-related information provided needs to be accurate and appropriate. Services need to be provided by people who are capable and qualified to do so. Health ministries need to be provided in a compassionate manner that reflects the beliefs and values of the congregation.

Licensed health professionals involved in health ministries are accountable to their licensing bodies to conduct themselves in a manner consistent with the standards of their profession. Parish nurses, and congregations with parish nurses, need to be aware that there are standards of practice for parish nursing that need to be followed.[11] Included in the standards are the expectation of both documentation and evaluation. While the standards are specific to nurses, they provide useful guidelines that could be adapted for other professionals serving as health ministers.

Insurance is another dimension of accountability. The church's insurance company should be informed of health ministries to be sure that the planned health ministry activities are covered in the church's policy. In addition, health professionals involved in health ministries should have liability insurance for their professional conduct. Liability insurance can be purchased independently or sometimes can be added to the church's policy or a homeowner's policy.

How will accountability be demonstrated to the congregation and people served through health ministries? For the congregation this can be demonstrated through verbal and written reports as well as behavior. Letting people in the church know what is happening through health ministries is an important responsibility. If people know what is happening and how it is having a positive impact, then they will be more likely to participate, support funding health ministries, and/or be willing to volunteer their time to help. The candle of health ministries should not be kept under a bushel.

Documentation reflects accountability. Keeping track of what happens through health ministries facilitates the ability to communicate with the congregation when the opportunity arises to share stories (with permission) or provide a report. Health ministry activities should be included in church annual reports that include information from different areas of ministry. Documentation also sets a professional standard for health ministry, and it enables the opportunity to evaluate effectiveness.

If health ministries provide one-to-one health related services, then a confidential written account needs to be kept. Information from the record can only be shared with permission, and any records should be kept in a locked cabinet with restricted access. How these records will be used needs to be explained to persons using the services, because record keeping, while essential in health care settings, is uncommon in the church setting.

It can also be helpful to document group activities. For example, when doing blood pressure screening, document how many people were screened and how many had high blood pressure. If health education is provided, document how many people participated and the approximate age range. This kind of information can be useful to share both with the congregation and with potential funders.

If partnership with other organizations is part of the health ministry, accountability to the partner for specific program expectations may be necessary. For example, in my previous position working for a hospital partnering with congregations, there was an expectation of a level of documentation from the churches necessary for the hospital's own evaluation and also required for external funders. Similarly, if the congregation receives any grants, there will be an expectation of accountability for how the funds are spent. Any documentation shared with partnering organizations needs to maintain client confidentiality.

FUTURE SUSTAINABILITY

Creating sustainable health ministries combines both the practical and the profound. It involves attention to the practical issues of accountability as well as the details of congregational life, and it involves responding to God's call to health, healing, and wholeness. Responsibly providing caring, compassionate, and competent service is good stewardship. Sustainable health ministries reflect these values. They are built on a firm foundation, have a clear mission and vision, are invigorated by the Holy Spirit, are supported by the congregation, are evaluated as meaningful by key stakeholders, and maintain a sense of integrity and accountability. The future of health ministries depends on cultivating these deep roots and expanding the vision for the church as a place of health and healing.

QUESTIONS FOR REFLECTION

1. How ready is this congregation to consider health ministries?
2. How could health ministry be connected to the mission and vision of this congregation?
3. What would be the areas of accountability for health ministries in this church?
4. How does this congregation evaluate its ministries?

IDEAS FOR CONGREGATIONAL ENGAGEMENT

1. Identify a long-standing health ministry in your region of the country and talk with that group about how their health ministry has been sustained. If you cannot find one, contact the Health Ministries Association (see Appendix C).
2. Start creating a vision for health ministries.

10

A VISION FOR THE FUTURE

The future holds many challenges and opportunities for those who would engage congregations in ministries of health. What we do, and how we do it, must be grounded in a theological understanding of health that is lived out practically in the life of the church, as we work responsibly to promote health, healing, and wholeness. We began our conversation talking about the significance of health ministry as a compound term that brings together health and ministry. As we look to the future, what does each of those strands have to offer? (See Figure 2.)

WEAVING HEALTH AND MINISTRY

On the health side the ability to document outcomes of services provided through ministries of health will be absolutely essential. These outcomes need to be quantifiable.[1] Practice in the health professions is based on research. Those in health care will be looking for solid research that documents the effectiveness of interventions provided in the church setting that differentiates this care from that offered in traditional health care settings. Health ministry programs supported by health care institutions will need outcome information for practice as well as continued financial support.

There also needs to be ongoing evaluation, both formal and informal, of the experience of people who use the services of a health minister. While the scope and standards of parish nursing

are specific to the nursing profession, the requirements for evaluation and research based practice would be beneficial to all
health ministers. In health care we speak of "patient satisfaction."
If the people being served experience a benefit that distinguishes
care received in the church from that provided in traditional
health care settings, they will support health ministries.

This information will be important for our health care
partners as well. As churches are seen as valuable and essential for community health initiatives rather than only convenient partners, they will become integral to future planning.
Health partners will recognize the value of supporting intentional ministries of health, and churches in turn will recognize
the value of faith and health partnerships.

Finally, health professionals serving as health ministers
not only need to have a sound educational preparation in their
clinical specialty, but they also need to be grounded in practical theology that informs their interdisciplinary practice as
much as their clinical knowledge. The church setting has

Figure 2: A Vision for the Future

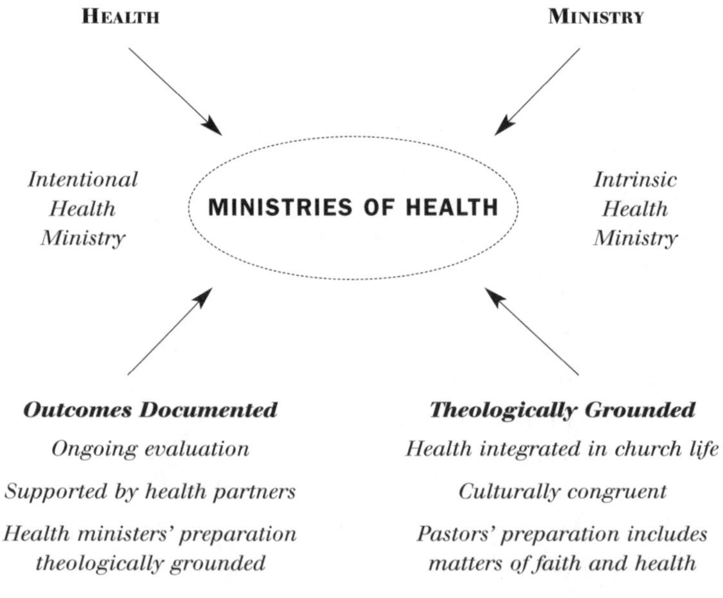

HEALTH   MINISTRY

Intentional Health Ministry   **MINISTRIES OF HEALTH**   *Intrinsic Health Ministry*

Outcomes Documented   ***Theologically Grounded***

Ongoing evaluation   *Health integrated in church life*

Supported by health partners   *Culturally congruent*

Health ministers' preparation theologically grounded   *Pastors' preparation includes matters of faith and health* fewer external controls than a health care setting, yet intentional health ministries need to be developed with the same integrity as health services provided in a clinical setting.

On the ministry side, ministries of health need to be theologically grounded, making them more than a program the church supports. Health needs to be integrated throughout the communal life of the church. Messages of the connection between faith and health need to be expressed in worship, in Christian education, in community outreach, and in fellowship opportunities, as well as through intentional health ministries. This integration of faith and health must be culturally congruent with the culture of the congregation, so what develops is a unique expression of church identity, values, and beliefs.

The intrinsic health ministry of the church that implicitly promotes health needs to be acknowledged and used in forming intentional health ministries. As the threads of health and ministry are woven together, each has valuable contributions to the future vision of ministries of health that wholeheartedly embrace the church's past, present, and future role in promoting health, healing, and wholeness. As churches around the country continue to weave health and ministry together, drawing on the strengths of each strand, they will create something stronger than either health or ministry could have formed alone.

EDUCATING FOR THE FUTURE

Seminaries need to contribute their support by educating future pastors to prepare their heads, their hearts, and their hands to support the health promoting possibilities of the church. Health professionals are by far the largest group within the Health Ministries Association. While there have been, and are, significant clergy leaders, health professionals have been in the forefront as the field has developed. The future is dependent on bringing more clergy and churches to the same level of commitment that many health professionals have experienced. When pastors are as likely as health professionals to say, "We need a health ministry in this church," then we will have come a long way.

For this to happen, the educational preparation of pastors needs to introduce them to matters of faith and health. Our seminary requires a spiritual formation course on embodiment that explores some of these themes for Masters of Divinity students. In addition, students can choose from a wide range of faith and health electives,[2] but it is the educational requirements that communicate implicitly what is seen as important. Without adding a burden to the curriculum, seminaries can be more mindful of supporting healthy and "wholly" living within their educational experience, and in so doing further the faith and health movement.[3] We can contribute to the health literacy of pastors through providing basic education and support in seminary life that hopefully can be extended into ministry.

After clergy leave seminary and go into ministry, denominations can continue to provide support for their wellness, as in fact some have done.[4] Those in ministry face particular challenges in self-care as a balance between body, mind, and spirit is sought. As pastors are supported to engage in life-affirming behaviors, they can bring their own experience to help support a ministry of health. The more personal connections pastors see between their own health and their faith, the greater the likelihood they will see the importance of ministries of health to the church.[5]

PROFESSIONAL DEVELOPMENT

Professional development for those involved in health ministries is critical to our future vision. This must include networking, formal and informal education, and denominational credentialing. As professional faith and health organizations grow in membership and resources, so will opportunities for continuing education, research, and support. The Health Ministries Association (HMA) is the broadest organization with a focus on congregationally based health ministries offering an annual conference with continuing education and opportunities for networking. Within HMA there are networks for parish nurses, health ministry coordinators, clergy, health education, lay health ministers, and faculty teaching health ministries in academic institutions. With parish nurses constituting the largest group, these networks represent the range of folks who are involved in the national development of health ministries. One of the wonderful things about being part of this field has been the opportunity to learn from other people of diverse backgrounds with a similar interest. The past has been characterized by a great openness to sharing among colleagues in health ministry that hopefully will continue in the future.

Two other membership organizations with a particular faith and health focus are the American Public Health Association's Caucus on Public Health and the Faith Community, which has a specific focus on public health, and the Christian Community Health Fellowship, which brings together folks committed to health care for the poor and provides supports for groups interested in developing faith-based health clinics around the country. Both of these groups are critical to supporting the role of the church in promoting healthy communities. As these professional associations supporting people serving in health ministries grow, they can enable a greater voice in the national discourse on health, and they can facilitate opportunities for sharing information and conducting research.

The future of health ministries will also require people with academic preparation in the field. While continuing education programs offer adequate preparation for what many will do in the church, the field also needs people with advanced degrees who can champion the cause, lead faith and health partnerships, direct health ministry programs, and conduct research. I firmly believe this preparation needs to include interdisciplinary learning, as people from diverse backgrounds are taught by faculty from diverse disciplines. The inherently interdisciplinary nature of health ministries requires that advanced education be interdisciplinary as well. My own work has been greatly enriched by perspectives from theology, public health, congregational studies, and community development. We need to be looking for other areas of knowledge that might contribute to health ministries, and we need to encourage people with diverse professional backgrounds to engage in our dialogue as well.

FINANCES

Developing adequate financial support will shape the future of health ministries. So much of what has developed in health ministries has used volunteers, and they have done many great things. In my own experience working with volunteers, I was impressed with the meaningful contributions these people made to their churches. While I believe we will always have people volunteering in health ministries, they still need adequate support to be effective, which requires leadership and costs money.

Recognizing that volunteers are important, the future of health ministries depends on valuing the role of health minister sufficiently that funds are found to hire a person. People in a paid position will have more time and energy to commit to nurturing ministries of health. Financial support in the church can best be generated by a firm theological foundation that articulates the vision for health ministries in the context of the church's mission and religious beliefs.[6] Ultimately I believe funding needs to come from the church because what we are doing is a ministry. While it may have components of hospital based community outreach, it is first and foremost a ministry.

When health ministries are part of improving the health of communities through faith and health partnerships, we need to engage other organizations with a vested interest, such as government health agencies and hospitals, to see how health ministries are consistent with their values and mission, and gain their financial support. An as yet uncharted possibility is to look at what services are provided through health ministries that may be billable.[7] Ultimately, the provision of ongoing support will be influenced by who has a sense of ownership for health ministries. When churches feel a strong sense of ownership and are able to do so, they will find the personal and financial resources to support the ministry. When public health departments value what churches bring to community health, they will find the financial resources to provide support. We also need to be open to future as yet unidentified partners that may emerge who want to share in this work.

While denominations are not providing salary support for health ministers, they are putting finances into developing health ministry resources and supporting their churches engaged in ministries of health. This kind of support is essential to the future. Denominations can do some of the theological and practical groundwork to facilitate churches' engagement in promoting health. In addition, as denominations find ways to officially recognize and credential health ministers, the value of this work to the life of the church will be affirmed.

There is a justice issue in creating a firm financial foundation for health ministries. We have seen that the church has been a valuable venue for providing services to those communities that are marginalized or have difficulty accessing traditional health care. Yet, churches with limited financial resources that might stand to benefit most from health ministries are the least likely to have the finances to support health ministries staff. Who can step up to share the burden? Some hospitals provide support as part of their community outreach, but this is often a vulnerable source of funding. As we come to understand more fully how the health of each of us is related to the health of all of us, we need to find ways to make health ministries not only possible in our own churches but in the churches of others who share an interest in faith and health but do not have adequate resources.

NEW TRENDS

Churches with fitness centers are an interesting recent development. The concept of Sports Ministry, although it is not emerging from congregationally based health ministries, has the potential to significantly influence the health of the church when the opportunities for active living are made easily available to the church and community.[8] Churches taking on the role of supporting active living can play an important role in improving the health of their communities and addressing our national obesity epidemic. On a smaller scale than a fitness center, I have seen churches with a room for fitness equipment to be used by members, and some offer gospel aerobics or walking programs. The more creatively and comprehensively churches think about what contributes to health, the more creative ministries of health will emerge.

Planting new churches offers another interesting possibility for the future, as health could be woven throughout congregational life from the beginning. I have not seen it done yet, but a new church plant could be developed with a mindset of promoting health.[9] This could be an interesting opportunity as a church is taking shape, to look at the intentional integration of themes of health, healing, and wholeness so it never becomes a separate program but is part of the fabric of emerging new church life and culture. Typically there is much that needs to be done to get a new church started, but what if the mindset was that this would be a church where the biblical message of health would be preached, where people would be encouraged to engage in life-affirming behaviors, where the communal life would be structured in ways that enhance the health of the group, and where those in need of healing could have their needs met? What would that look like?

LANGUAGE FOR THE FUTURE

A vision for the future will include language that clearly articulates to health professionals, clergy, and church members why promoting health is fundamental to church life. Without becoming obsessed with semantics we need to recognize that language is power. We need to use this influence when articulating a vision for health ministries for the church, sponsoring organizations, and partners. The power of health ministry language will be in part dependent on the cultural understanding of the congregation. All churches cannot be expected to know intuitively that promoting health is integral to church life. We need to be able to effectively communicate why this is the case using language that is culturally appropriate to each church and its tradition. The ability to use language to effectively communicate with our churches increases the likelihood that we will be understood, and that meaningful ministries will emerge.

How can we express the practical and the profound dimensions of health ministries in words that speak to clergy and health professionals, as well as congregations? This can happen only through concerted effort on the part of all involved to listen to different perspectives as a common ground and a shared language are sought. Shaping the language for the future will involve trying to understand diverse perspectives of health professionals, clergy, and lay people as the meaning of the church as a place of health and healing is explored. Translators who can bridge multiple perspectives will be needed as the language of the church's intentional health ministries is integrated with the language of intrinsic health ministry to express the wholeness of the church's role in health. Like the facets of a prism, our language can be enhanced by insight from multiple fields and theological perspectives as the interdisciplinary work of health ministries grow.

HEALTHY LIVING FOR THE FUTURE

Being involved in health ministries changes lives. It changes the lives of the people receiving and it changes the lives of the people giving. For health ministries to reach their full potential, those of us in leadership need to be personally transformed, knowing in our hearts as well as our heads that body/mind/spirit are inseparable and that faith and health are joined as one chord in the song of life. Our lives need to model what we preach and teach. Nothing but the transforming love of Christ can make this happen as we seriously try to walk the talk.

This transformation needs to extend beyond individuals and the walls of our churches to our neighborhoods as well. I would hope for a future where churches engaging in ministries of health would not only nurture the well-being of their members, but also reach out to their communities and share in the task of making their neighborhoods healthy, life-affirming places. I would hope for a future where churches would be as likely to engage in acts of justice to right wrongs that keep people from being healthy, as they are to engage in acts of compassion and mercy to help folks when they are ill.

Our vision for the future of health ministries must not be limited by the past. We may continue to see current models of health ministry play a significant role but we must also be open to new ways congregations might promote health that have yet to be imagined. The future vision of the church as a place of health and healing will depend on the innovative use of existing models of health ministry, and a creative eye toward the future to develop new faith and health paradigms as churches, society, and culture change. We need to be solidly rooted in our church's theological traditions, informed of the existing health ministry paradigms, and open to future possibilities that could take us in ways as yet unimagined. The future will be shaped by creative individuals and committed churches responding to the call to engage in ministries of health.

APPENDIX A

Congregational Assessment Guide

Whether you are working with an unfamiliar congregation or one where you are a member, you need to be consciously attentive to what happens in the congregation and what the members think and feel about health, healing, and health ministry. Working through the information in this guide will help lay the groundwork for developing or expanding health ministries in your particular congregation. Some of the questions you will answer through your own observations, other questions will require talking to people within the congregation. The assessment is intended to provide a cognitive map, a way of thinking, as you explore the possibilities for health ministry with a particular congregation.

The content areas of the assessment are based on areas I have found to be significant in my work with congregations. An individual or health ministry team working with a congregation on ministries of health may want to use this guide as a way of working through an understanding of the unique congregational culture. A program coordinator working with multiple congregations will not have the time or ability to accumulate this depth of information, but will find the general areas of consideration useful in program development work. If you are working with a congregation that already has health ministries, the guide may reveal some areas where additional information could be helpful.

Note: Before beginning the process of congregational assessment you will want to have the consent of the pastor and any congregational leadership group to gather information for developing health ministries, respecting when information needs to be kept in confidence.

SOURCES OF INFORMATION

There are several different sources of information for learning about congregational culture.

- Attend worship services. What is the atmosphere? What is happening in the services? Who is participating? What symbols and rituals are used, and what is their meaning?

- Attend social events of the congregation. Who is there? What is the atmosphere? What kind of food, if any, is served? Is this event a place where health issues are addressed or could be addressed?

- Attend committee meetings. Two committee areas you would want to have contact with are the committees that deal with issues of care for the congregation and community outreach. What issues are being discussed? How are decisions made? Who are key leaders? How, if at all, do these committees' work contribute to wholistic health?

- Read written materials: Sunday bulletins, newsletters, annual reports, minutes of relevant committee meetings, documents of church history.

- Talk with a wide variety of people, including clergy, church staff, church secretary, active lay people such as members of the congregation's governing body, finance committee, and leaders of groups (e.g., women, men, youth).

HEALTH

If you want to develop health ministries in a congregation, it is important to understand what health means to members of the congregation and what connections, if any, they see between faith and health. These questions are intended to be asked of individuals.

- What does being healthy mean to you?

- Do you experience a connection between your faith and your health, and if you do, can you tell me about that connection?

- There has been a lot of medical research showing that people who attend worship services regularly are healthier and live longer. Why do you think that might be?

CHRISTIAN HISTORY AND TRADITION IN HEALTH MINISTRIES

- What resources, such as archives, publications, or people are available for learning about the history of this congregation?

- Does this congregation have a history of involvement in issues of health? Healing? Medical missions?

- Are there any significant events or issues in the history of this congregation that would impact the development or expansion of ministries of health?

- What stories of church life are often repeated by members of this congregation? And what values do they reflect?

- Are there any dynamics in recent history that influence the potential for health ministries in this church?

CONGREGATIONAL CULTURE

The following questions provide a guide for learning about congregational culture. An effort needs to be made to understand as much as you can about the culture to develop sensitivity and be able to create health ministries congruent with the culture of the congregation with which you are working. Some of these questions you may ask people and others you may answer through your own observations.

Religion

- What are key religious beliefs for this congregation? How could these key beliefs be incorporated into health ministries?

- Is this congregation part of a denomination, and if so, is it a strong affiliation?

- Are there denominational resources for health ministries?

- Are there any texts, in addition to the Bible, that are important to this congregation? If so, what do they say about health and healing?

- What religious rituals and traditions in this congregation are related to health and healing?

Social Context

- What are the existing family structures within the congregation? What implication does this have for health ministry? If a health ministry is already in place, have families been incorporated into health ministries?
- What are key groups within the congregation?
- Who are key people within this congregation who could help you understand it better?
- What are the patterns of gathering for this congregation? That is, when can you find people together in groups?
- What is the role of women in this congregation and how might that influence the development of health ministries?
- How is the profession of nursing perceived within this congregation (this is significant if parish nursing is a model of health ministry your congregation is considering)?

Cultural Values

- What does this congregation value (i.e., what is considered important)?
- How does this congregation care for its members?
- How does this congregation care for people outside of its membership?
- What health issues are of concern to this congregation? If a health ministry is already in place, to what health issues have members been particularly responsive?

Ethnicity

- What cultural groups are represented within this congregation? Within the surrounding neighborhood?
- How do the different cultural groups interact?
- Are there any cultural issues that should be considered in developing health ministries?

Politics and Legal Issues

- How do external politics affect what happens within this congregation?

- How do internal politics affect what happens within this congregation?
- What legal issues would be important for this congregation to consider in developing health ministries?

Economics

- How would you describe the economic status of members of this congregation?
- What church activities are given priority in the budget?
- Are financial issues a concern for this congregation? If so, how would that impact the development of health ministries?

Education

- What role does education have in the life of this congregation?
- How might health ministries be integrated into the existing patterns of education?
- What are the educational backgrounds of members of this congregation? How might this shape how health ministries should be developed?
- What educational opportunities are provided in this congregation? How might health be integrated into existing educational offerings?

Environmental Context

- Describe the neighborhood of this congregation. How does the neighborhood impact the possibilities and need for health ministries?
- Is the building handicapped accessible?
- Are there environmental issues in the church building or neighborhood?

Language

- What languages are spoken within this congregation?
- What religious language is used by this congregation?

- What words and concepts might this congregation use to describe health, healing, and health ministry?
- Is this a congregation of oral or written tradition? If oral, with whom do you need to talk? If written, what is available that you can read?

Technology

- How is technology used in this congregation?
- Are there ways that technology could be used for health ministries?

CONGREGATIONAL AND COMMUNITY STRENGTHS

The strengths of the congregation and the community provide important building blocks for health ministries.

- In what areas is this congregation particularly effective? How might these areas of strength be used in developing health ministries?
- What resources (people, organizations, building, finances) does this congregation have that could be used in developing health ministries?
- What are the strengths of the community surrounding the church? How might these areas of strength be used in developing health ministries?
- What resources (people, agencies, programs) does the community have that could be used in developing or expanding health ministries?

THE CHURCH'S ROLE IN PROMOTING HEALTHY COMMUNITIES

Understanding and affirming what the congregation is already doing that has a positive impact on health is an important part of developing health ministries. The following questions, to be discussed with congregation members, are designed to address this topic.

- Can you tell me any ways that your participation in this congregation is good for your health? Are there any ways that your participation in this congregation is bad for your health? If yes, please explain.

- Can you tell me about any times that health or healing issues have been addressed in worship services, in Christian education, or other church programs? If your congregation has an organized health ministry, have there been any health activities at church that you have found particularly helpful or meaningful?

- Is there anything you would like to see this congregation do to promote health?

- In what church settings do you feel most connected to other church members?

- How might the Healthy People 2010 goals of increasing quality and years of healthy life and eliminating health disparities motivate this congregation to engage in ministries of health?

FAITH AND HEALTH PARTNERSHIPS

- What, if any, health related organizations (hospitals, clinics, department of health, home health agencies, etc.,) in your congregation's community are currently involved in health ministries?

- What health related organizations might be potential partners for your congregation in health ministries?

- Are there other congregations in the community that might be interested in collaborative health ministries?

- Does this church have any history of partnering with other groups? Would those experiences influence any new faith and health partnerships?

MODELS OF HEALTH MINISTRY

- What is this congregation's vision for health ministry and is there an existing model consistent with that vision that would be appropriate for this church? Is there a new model that could be created that would be more suitable?

- What approaches to health ministry exist within your community?

RESOURCES FOR HEALTH MINISTRY

- Of the available resources for developing health ministry, which would be most appropriate for this congregation? Why?

BUILDING SUSTAINABLE HEALTH MINISTRIES

- How is the congregation organized (both members and staff)?
- What groups and/or committees are involved in activities that promote health?
- What church groups and/or committees would be logical partners for health ministries?
- Who visits people that are sick or unable to get out?
- What congregational support needs to be developed in order to ensure the continuation of health ministries?
- How does this church evaluate its programs and ministry?

APPENDIX B

Health Ministry Resources

FAITH AND HEALTH MEMBERSHIP ORGANIZATIONS

Health Ministries Association
295 West Crossville Road, Suite 130
Roswell, GA 30075
800-280-9919
www.hmassoc.org

HMA has an annual conference in June and local chapters in different regions of the country. The website has a listing of health ministry resources from various denominations. Resources can be purchased, including a Health Ministry Program Manual, *Scope and Standards of Parish Nursing Practice,* and *Walking in the Way,* a guide for developing a faith-based walking program.

American Public Health Association
Caucus on Public Health and the Faith Community
800 I Street NW
Washington, DC 20001-3710
202-777-2742
www.apha.org

APHA has an annual conference in November. Information about abstracts presented at past conferences are available on the website.

Christian Community Health Fellowship
3812 W. Ogden Ave.
Chicago, IL 60623
773-277-2243
www.cchf.org

CCHF has an annual conference in May. The website has a listing of best practices in faith-based health centers.

OTHER FAITH AND HEALTH ORGANIZATIONS

Interfaith Health Program
Rollins School of Public Health
Emory University
760 Commerce Street
Decataur, GA 30030
404-592-1461
www.ihpnet.org

The IHP website has papers on faith and health and links to other useful websites. The organization also has a faith and health list serve.

International Parish Nurse Resource Center
475 E. Lockwood
St. Louis, MO 63119
314-918-2527
http://ipnrc.parishnurses.org/

The IPNRC holds the annual Westberg Symposium for parish nurses in September.

BOOKS ABOUT HEALTH MINISTRIES

Evans, Abigail Rian. *Healing Church: Practical Programs for Health Ministries.* United Church Press, 1999.
Gunderson, Gary. *Deeply Woven Roots.* Minneapolis: Fortress Press, 1997.
Knaist, Robert, and Larry Seidl. *Partners in Healing.* St. Louis: Catholic Health Care Association, 1997.

BOOKS FOR INDIVIDUAL OR GROUP STUDY

Beckmen, Richard. *Praying for Wholeness and Healing.* Minneapolis: Augsberg, 1995.
Clinebell, Howard. *Anchoring Your Well-Being: Christian Wholeness in a Fractured World.* Nashville: Upper Room, 1997.
Hesson, Margie. *Stress Less.* Nashville: Abingdon, 1999.
_____. *Health Yourself.* Nashville: Abingdon, 1995.

Koch, Carl, and Joyce Heil. *God Knows You'd Like a New Body.* Notre Dame, Ind.: Sorin Books, 2001.

Paulsell, Stephanie. *Honoring the Body.* San Francisco: Jossey-Bass, 2002.

Tubesing, Donald, and Nancy Tubesing. *Seeking Your Healthy Balance.* Duluth, Minn.: Whole Person Associates, 1991.

RESOURCES FOR INTEGRATING FAITH AND HEALTH IN CHURCH LIFE

Evans, Abigail Rian. *Healing Liturgies for the Seasons of Life.* Louisville: Westminster John Knox Press, 2004.

Kirk-Duggan, Cheryl. *The Undivided Soul: Helping Congregations Connect Body and Spirit.* Nashville: Abingdon, 2001.

APPENDIX C

Litany of Health and Healing

LEADER: Lord, when we praise you, experiencing our connection with the source of all life,

ALL: **We promote health and healing.**

LEADER: Lord, when we praise you with glorious music,

ALL: **We promote health and healing.**

LEADER: Lord, when we study your Word, learning more about what it means to be a Christian,

ALL: **We promote health and healing.**

LEADER: Lord, when we pray for one another,

ALL: **We promote health and healing.**

LEADER: Lord, when we experience the fellowship of belonging to a community of faith,

ALL: **We promote health and healing.**

LEADER: Lord, when we support and encourage health professionals in our congregation,

ALL: **We promote health and healing.**

LEADER: Lord, when we share the journey of chronic illness with others,

ALL: **We promote health and healing.**

LEADER: Lord, when we share the journey of grief with others,

ALL: **We promote health and healing.**

Dear God, who yearns to make each of us whole, we claim and affirm the many ways in which our congregation is already a place of health and healing. We also claim and affirm the potential of our community of faith to be an even greater source of health and healing. May we capture your vision today of a healing ministry for our church that can restore health and wholeness to both our congregation and the community we serve. In the name of your son Jesus Christ, who came to heal us all. Amen.

AUTHOR'S NOTE: I created this litany to highlight the intrinsic health ministry in my own church. Feel free to adapt it to your own congregation.

NOTES

CHAPTER ONE

1. Jeff Levin, *God, Faith and Health* (New York: Wiley, 2001).

2. Portions of this section were originally published in Mary Chase-Ziolek, "Rethinking our Terms: Health Ministry or Ministry of Health?" *Journal of Christian Nursing* (Spring 2003): 21–22.

3. See Edward Hall, *Beyond Culture* (New York: Doubleday, 1976).

4. Mary Chase-Ziolek and Madelyn Iris, "Nurses' Perspectives on the Distinctive Aspects of Providing Nursing Care in a Congregational Setting," *Journal of Community Health Nursing* (2002): 173–86.

5. Pamela Couture, "When Public Health and Faith Groups Encounter Each Other: Overcoming Obstacles," available online at http://www.ihpnet.org/couturetxt.htm (accessed June 19, 2004).

6. Mary Chase-Ziolek, "The Meaning and Experience of Health Ministry within the Culture of a Congregation with a Parish Nurse," *Transcultural Nursing* (1999): 49–50.

7. For an excellent resource of healing liturgies, see Abigail Rian Evans, *Healing Liturgies for the Seasons of Life* (Louisville: Westminster John Knox Press, 2004).

CHAPTER TWO

1. Gary Gunderson, *Deeply Woven Roots: Improving the Quality of Life in Your Community* (Minneapolis: Fortress Press, 1997), 4.

2. For a thorough study of the Bible and health, see John Wilkinson, *The Bible and Healing: A Medical and Theological Commentary* (Grand Rapids: Eerdmans, 1998).

3. Ibid., 16–17.

4. Ibid., 13–14.

5. Justice in matters of health continues to be a central concern of public health and of liberation theology. See Alastair Campbell, *Health as Liberation: Medicine, Theology, and the Quest for Justice* (Cleveland: Pilgrim Press, 1995).

6. John Pilch, *Healing in the New Testament: Insights from Medieval and Mediterranean Anthropology* (Minneapolis: Fortress Press, 2000), 8–9.

7. I am indebted to my colleague Jim Bruckner, associate professor of Old Testament at North Park Theological Seminary, for his understanding of nephesh.

8. Wilkonson, *The Bible and Healing,* 11–12.

9. Paul Tillich, *The Meaning of Health* (Chicago: Exploration Press, 1984), 17.

10. Stephen Schmidt, "Health and Salvation: Musings on Meanings," *Religious Education* (1994): 170–72.

11. Ralph Underwood, "God's Life-Giving Ways: Practical Principles for Healing Ministry," *Insights* (Spring 1999): 8.

12. Thomas Droege, "Congregations as Communities of Health and Healing," *Interpretation* (April 1995): 118.

13. Evangelical Lutheran Church of America, *Our Ministry of Healing Health and Health Care Today* (Chicago: ELCA, 2001), 21–22.

14. Presbyterian Church U.S.A., *Life Abundant: Values, Choices and Health Care: the Responsibility and Role of the Presbyterian Church U.S.A.* (Louisville, Ky.: The Office of the General Assembly, The Presbyterian Church U.S.A., 1988), 42.

15. United Church of Christ, "Resolution Reclaiming the Church's Role in Health and Healing," available online at http://www.ucc.org/justice/health/resolution.htm (accessed June 19, 2004).

16. Abigail Rian Evans, *Redeeming Marketplace Medicine* (Cleveland: Pilgrim Press, 1999), 63.

17. James Wind, *A Letter on Peace and Good Health* (Minneapolis: Lutheran Brotherhood, 1998), 13.

18. Leo Thomas and Jan Alkire, *Healing as a Parish Ministry* (Notre Dame, Ind.; Ave Maria Press, 1992), 46.

19. James Evans, "Health, Disease, and Salvation in African American Experience," *Princeton Seminary Bulletin* (1996): 344.

20. The Christian Medical Commission, *Healing and Wholeness: The Churches' Role in Health* (Geneva, Switzerland: World Council of Churches, 1990), 6.

21. Dr. Meleis is a nurse scholar. This quote is found in Mary Huch, "Perspectives on Health," *Nursing Science Quarterly* (1991): 34.

22. This definition from the World Health Organization can be found online at http://www.who.int/about/definition/en/ (accessed May 10, 2004).

23. Afaf Meleis, "Being and Becoming Healthy: The Core of Nursing Knowledge," *Nursing Science Quarterly* (1990): 110.

24. Droege, "Congregations as Communities of Health," 117–28.

25. Abigail Rian Evans, "The Church as an Institution of Health," *Interpretation* (April 1995): 161–68.

26. Daniel Fountain, *New Paradigms in Christian Health Ministries* (Brunswick, Ga.: MAP International, 2001), 2.

27. United Methodist Church, *Congregational Health Ministries: A Guide for Congregations* (New York: UMC, 1997), ii.

28. Wendell Berry, "Health is Membership," available online at http://www.tipiglen.dircon.co.uk/berryhealth.html (accessed June 19, 2004).

29. Underwood, "God's Live-Giving Ways," 11.

CHAPTER THREE

1. Morton Kelsey's *Healing & Christianity* (Minneapolis: Augsburg, 1995) provides an exhaustive study of the history of the church in health and healing.

2. Pamela Couture, "Partners in Healing: Bridging Pastoral Care and Public Health through Practical and Pastoral Theology," *Journal of Pastoral Theology* (Summer 1995): 66.

3. *Healing and Wholeness: The Churches' Role in Health* is available through the Health Ministries Association, 980 Canton Street, Building 1, Suite B, Roswell, GA 30075, 800-280-9919.

4. David Zersen, "Parish Nursing: 20th-Century Fad?" *Journal of Christian Nursing* (Spring 1994): 37–40.

5. Joan Newsome, "Nurses in the African American Church," *ABNF Journal* (1994): 134–7.

6. See Granger Westberg, *Theological Roots of Wholistic Health Care* (Hinsdale, Ill.: Wholistic Health Centers, 1979).

7. Granger Westberg "A Personal Historical Perspective," in Phyllis Ann Solari-Twadell and Mary Ann McDermott, *Parish Nursing: Promoting Whole Person Health Within Faith Communities* (Thousand Oaks, Ca.: Sage, 1999), 35–41.

8. John Hatch, Anne Cunningham, Wanda Woods, and Felicia Snipes, "The Fitness Through Churches Project," *Hygie* (1986): 9–12.

9. Larry Dossey's books include such titles as *Meaning and Medicine* (New York: Bantam, 1991), *Healing Words* (San Francisco: Harper, 1993), and *Prayer Is Good Medicine* (New York: Harper Collins, 1997).

10. David Edelberg, "Making Room for Alternatives: An Interview with David Edelberg," *Second Opinion* (1994): 20–33.

11. For a thoughtful discussion of the church's role in health care see the Evangelical Lutheran Church in America's document *Our Ministry of Healing Health and Health Care Today* (Chicago: ELCA, 2001).

12. Contact the Faith Project of the Universal Health Care Action Network at 2800 Euclid Ave., Suite 520, Cleveland, OH 44115, 216-241-8422, or http://www.uhcan.org/faith/index.html.

13. Joanne Olson, Jane Simington, and Margaret Clark, "Educating Parish Nurses," *Canadian Nurse* (1998): 40–44.

14. Anne vanLoon, "The Development of Faith Community Nursing Programs as a Response to Changing Australian Health Policy," *Health Education & Behavior* (1998): 790–9.

15. Mary Chase-Ziolek and Madelyn Iris, "Nurses' Perspectives on the Distinctive Aspects of Providing Nursing Care in a Congregational Setting," *Journal of Community Health Nursing* (Fall 1998): 173–86.

16. Caswell Evans, "The Faith and Public Health Partnership," *Our Connecting Point* (1995): 1–2.

17. William Foege, "What Is Our Task in Health?" in *The Challenges of Faith and Health* (Atlanta: Carter Center, 1994), 27–28.

18. Thomas Droege, "Congregations as Communities of Health and Healing," *Interpretation* (April 1995): 121–22.

19. Daniel Fountain, *New Paradigms in Christian Health Ministries* (Brunswick, Ga.: MAP International, 2001), 2–3.

20. Lyle Schaller, *Innovations in Ministry* (Nashville: Abingdon Press, 1994), 18–36.

21. A listing of denominational resources for health ministries can be found on the Health Ministries Association web page at http://www.hmassoc.org (accessed June 19, 2004).

CHAPTER FOUR

1. Madeline Leininger, *Culture Care Diversity and Universality: A Theory of Nursing* (New York: NLN, 1991), 47.

2. Nancy Ramsay, "The Congregation as a Culture; Implications for Ministry," *Encounter* (1992): 36–40.

3. Martin Marty, "The Congregation as a Culture," *Christian Ministry* (January–February 1991): 15.

4. James Wind and James Lewis, *American Congregations: Volume One: Portraits of Twelve Religious Communities* (Chicago: University of Chicago Press, 1994), 2–3.

5. Carl Dudley and David Roozen, *Faith Communities Today* (Hartford, Ct.: Hartford Seminary, March 2001), 15.

6. See the Dudley and Roozen report for a full discussion of congregational identity. Available online at http://fact.hartsem.edu (accessed June 19, 2004).

7. Nancy Ammerman, "Culture and Identity in the Congregation," in Nancy Ammerman, Jackson Carroll, Carl Dudley, and William McKinney, *Studying Congregations* (Nashville: Abingdon Press, 1998), 81.

8. Carl Dudley and Sally Johnson, *Energizing the Congregation* (Louisville: Westminister John Knox Press, 1993).

9. David Roozen, William McKinney, and Jackson Carroll, *Varieties of Religious Presence* (New York: Pilgrim Press, 1984).

10. Ramsay, "Congregation as a Culture," 38.

11. James Spradley, *Participant Observation* (Fort Worth, Tex.: Harcourt Brace Jovanovich, 1980).

12. Gary Gunderson, "Backing onto Sacred Ground," *Public Health Reports* (2000): 261.

13. For a full discussion of culture and health care see Rachel Spector, *Cultural Diversity in Health and Illness* (Stamford, Conn.: Appleton Lange, 1996).

CHAPTER FIVE

1. Jody Kretzmann and John McKnight, *Building Communities from the Inside Out* (Chicago: ACTA Publications, 1993).

2. John McKnight, "Strengthening Communities from the Inside Out," Chicago Area Schweitzer Fellows Program, December 2, 2003.

3. Kretzmann and McKnight, *Building Communities*, 13.

4. David Hilfiker, "The Limits of Charity," *The Other Side* (2000): 4.

5. John McKnight, *The Careless Society* (New York: Basic Books, 1995).

6. Gary Gunderson, *Deeply Woven Roots* (Minneapolis: Fortress, 1997), 22.

7. Kretzmann and McKnight, *Building Communities*, 143–60.

8. Westberg, "A Personal Historical Perspective," in Phyllis Ann Solari-Twadell and Mary Ann McDermott, *Parish Nursing: Promoting Whole Person Health within Faith Communities* (Thousand Oaks, Cal.: Sage, 1999), 40–41.

9. See Deborah Patterson, *The Essential Parish Nurse* (Cleveland: Pilgrim Press, 2003), for a sample congregational survey.

10. Janalou Blecke and Lisa Hadden, "Community Defined Health; Thinking from the Inside Out," *Metropolitan Universities* (2000), 41.

CHAPTER SIX

1. Portions of this chapter were published in Mary Chase-Ziolek, "The Transforming Power of the Church to Promote Community Health," *Covenant Quarterly* (August 2003): 29–41.

2. In 2001 the United States spent $251.2 billion on hospital care, $140.6 billion on prescription drugs, and only $46.4 billion on government public health activities. From Center for Disease Control, Health

United States 2003, table 115, http://www.cdc.gov/nchs/products/ pubs/pubd/hus/trendtables.htm, accessed April 3, 2004.

3. United Methodist Church, *Health for All Manual* (New York: UMC, 1997), discusses how churches can address individual, family, congregational, community, and national health.

4. Mary Chase-Ziolek, "The Meaning and Experience of Health Ministry within the Culture of a Congregation with a Parish Nurse," *Transcultural Nursing* (1999): 49–50.

5. Afaf Meleis, "Being and Becoming Health: The Core of Nursing Knowledge," *Nursing Science Quarterly* (Summer 1990): 109–10.

6. Patricia Nafzger, "Congregational Assessment," unpublished paper, North Park Theological Seminary, Chicago, Illinois, May 2002.

7. Jeff Levin, *God, Faith and Health* (New York: Wiley, 2001), 13.

8. Joel Shulman and Keith Meador, *Heal Thyself* (Oxford, U.K.: Oxford University Press, 2003), 45.

9. National Health Observance calendar, http://www.healthfinder .gov/library/nho/nho.asp.

10. Jane Peterson, Jan Atwood, and Bernice Yates, "Key Elements for Church-Based Health Promotion Programs: Outcome-Based Literature Review, *Public Health Nursing* (November/December 2002): 401–10.

11. Frances Stillman, Lee Bone, Cynthia Rand, David Levine, and Diane Becker, "Heart, Body, and Soul: A Church-Based Smoking-Cessation Program for African Americans," *Preventive Medicine* (1993): 335–49.

12. John Hatch and Steve Derthick, "Empowering Black Churches for Health Promotion," *Health Values* (1992): 3–9.

13. James Wind, *A Letter on Peace and Good Health* (Minneapolis: Lutheran Brotherhood, 1998), 16.

14. Institute of Medicine, *The Future of Public Health* (Washington: National Academy Press, 1988).

15. The United Church of Christ has suggestions for churches working with Healthy People 2010 goals online at http://www.ucc.org/justice/ health/healthy_people.htm, accessed May 10, 2004.

16. David Hilton, "Bringing About Real Health," *Health & Development* (1993): 21–24. More information on Transformation for Health can be found at http://www.globalhealthaction.org.

CHAPTER SEVEN

1. Public Health in Parish Nursing Program, Frederick County Health Department, 350 Montevue Lane, Frederick, MD 21702, 301-631-3360, http://www.frederickhealth.org/nursing/parish/index.htm.

2. California Department of Health Services 5 A Day Faith Based Project, Department of Health Services, Cancer Prevention & Nutrition Section, 16161 Capitol Ave., Suite 74.516 MS 7204, Sacramento, CA 95899-7413, 916-449-5430, http://www.dhs.ca.gov/ps/cdic/cpns/aa/faith.htm.

3. National Center for Cultural Competence, Sharing a Legacy of Caring Partnerships between Health Care and Faith-Based Organizations (Washington, D.C.: Author, 2001).

4. U.S. Department of Health and Human Services, Healthy People 2010, http://www.healthypeople.gov/document/html/uih/uih_1.htm, accessed May 10, 2004.

5. Rev. Delois Brown-Daniels, keynote address, Journey Toward Wellness conference of Advocate Health Care, Downers Grove, Illinois, December 2, 2003.

6. Paul Mattessich, Marta Murray-Close, and Barbara Monsey, *Collaboration: What Makes it Work* (St. Paul, Minn.: Wilder Foundation, 2001), 61.

7. Drucker Foundation, *Meeting the Collaboration Challenge* (San Francisco: Josey-Bass, 2002), 54.

8. See Centers for Disease Control and Prevention, *Engaging Faith Communities as Partners in Improving Community Health* (Atlanta: CDC, 1999).

9. National Center for Cultural Competence, *Sharing a Legacy,* 23–24.

10. Mattessich et al., *Collaboration,* 8–9.

11. Deaconess Foundation Parish Nurse Ministries, 211 N. Broadway, Suite 1260, St. Louis, MO 63102, 314-436-8001, http://www .deaconess .org/dpmm.asp.

12. Queens Care Faith and Health Partnership, 4618 Fountain Ave., Suite 102, Los Angeles, CA 90029, 323-644-6180, http://www.queenscare .org/healthandfaith.html.

13. Pamela Couture, "Partners in Healing: Bridging Pastoral Care and Public Health Through Practical and Pastoral Theology," *Journal of Pastoral Theology* (Summer 1995): 65–67.

14. To find a complete listing of the presentations at past American Public Health Association meetings, go to http://www.apha.org/meetings. Under past meetings search for Caucus on the Public Health and Faith Community.

15. Your local American Heart Association can be reached by calling 1-800-242-8721.

16. The Witness Project, Arkansas Cancer Research Center, 4301 West Markham, Slot 629 A, Little Rock, AR 72205, 501-686-8801, http://www.acrc.uams.edu/patients/WitnessProject/index.html.

17. Balm in Gilead, 130 West 42nd St. Suite 450, New York, NY 10036, 212-730-7381, http://www.balmingilead.org/home.asp.

CHAPTER EIGHT

1. Jill Westberg McNamara, *The Health Cabinet* (Park Ridge, Ill.: International Parish Nurse Resource Center, 1997), 12–13.

2. Jack Lundin, "Introduction to the First Edition," in McNamara, *Health Cabinet,* 5.

3. Phone conversation with Alvyne Rethemeyer, director of the International Parish Nurse Resource Center, May 5, 2004.

4. Mary Chase-Ziolek and Jan Striepe, "A Comparison of Urban versus Rural Experiences of Nurses Volunteering to Promote Health in Churches," *Public Health Nursing* (August 1999): 273–76.

5. Health Ministries Association/American Nurses Association. *Scope and Standards of Parish Nursing Practice* (Washington, D.C.: ANA, 1998).

6. Peggy Matteson, "Parish Nursing–A New, Yet Old Model of Care," *Massachusetts Nurse* (March 1, 1999), 5.

7. There is a series of books with brief health educational articles that health ministers can use called *Seasons for Wholeness,* available through the International Parish Nurse Resource Center at http://www.parishnurses.org/. You can also sign up for a monthly email list from Wheat Ridge Foundation that will give you similar material: http://www.wheatridge.org/.

8. National Institutes of Health: http://www.nih.gov/.

9. This website from Purdue University provides guidelines for discerning the quality of information on the internet: http://www.lib.purdue.edu/ugrl/staff/sharkey/interneteval/ (accessed June 19, 2004).

10. Diane Conrad, "Team Nursing in Parish Nurse Ministry: Even Jesus Had Twelve Disciples," Westberg Symposium (September 1995).

11. Mary Chase-Ziolek and Jo Ann Gruca, "Clients' Perceptions of Distinctive Aspects of Nursing Care Received within a Congregational Setting," *Journal of Community Health Nursing* (Fall 2000): 171–83.

12. Mary Chase-Ziolek and Madelyn Iris, "Nurses' Perspectives on the Distinctive Aspects of Providing Nursing Care in a Congregational Setting," *Journal of Community Health Nursing* (Fall 2002): 177–79.

13. Chase-Ziolek and Gruca, 177.

14. Chase-Ziolek and Iris, 177–78.

15. Gail Price, a physical therapist, has been serving as minister of health at Ascension Lutheran Church in Northbrook, Illinois, since 1993.

16. Robert Wood Johnson Foundation, "Development of Community Health Advisor Networks in the Southeastern United States," available online at http://www.rwjf.org/reports/grr/029271s.htm (accessed May 10, 2004).

17. National Rural Health Association, "Community Health Advisor Programs," available online at http://www.nrharural.org/dc/issue papers/ipaper17.html (accessed May 10, 2004).

18. W. Daniel Hale and Richard Bennett, *Building Healthy Communities Through Medical-Religious Partnerships* (Baltimore: John Hopkins Press, 2000), 131.

19. Church Health Services, 308 Oneida St., Beaver Dam, WI 53916, 920-887-1766, http://www.churchclinic.org.

20. Christian Community Health Fellowship, 3812 W. Ogden Ave., Chicago, IL 60623, 773-843-2700, http://www.cchf.org.

21. Association of Brethren Caregivers, *The Lafiya Guide* (Elgin, Ill.: ABC, 1993), 11.

22. Stephen's Ministries, 2045 Innerbelt Business Center Dr., St. Louis, MO 63114, 314-428-2600, http://www.stephenministries.org/.

23. Befriender's Ministry, 2260 Summit Ave., St. Paul, MN 55105, 651-962-5775, http://www.stthomas.edu/bef/.

24. See Universal Health Care Action Network (UHCAN), *Seeking Justice in Health Care* (Cleveland: Author, 2004), for a guide for advocates in faith communities.

25. Abigail Rian Evans, *The Healing Church Practical Programs for Health Ministries* (Cleveland: United Church Press, 1999), 70–92.

CHAPTER NINE

1. Health Ministries Association, *A Guide to Developing a Health Ministry* (Roswell, Ga.: Author, 2002), is a useful resource when starting.

2. Renae Schumann and Dale Mannon, "Weaving the Effective Congregational Health Ministry," *Oates Journal* 3 (2000): 3–4.

3. For more worship resources, see Cheryl Kirk-Duggan, *The Undivided Soul: Helping Congregations Connect Body and Spirit* (Nashville: Abingdon, 2001).

4. Mary Chase-Ziolek and Jan Striepe, "A Comparison of Urban versus Rural Experiences of Nurses Volunteering to Promote Health in Churches," *Public Health Nursing* (1999): 279.

5. Mary Chase-Ziolek and Madelyn Iris, "Nurses' Perspectives on the Distinctive Aspects of Providing Nursing Care in a Congregational Setting," *Journal of Community Health Nursing* (Fall 2002): 179.

6. Susan Fuentes, "Program Evaluation," in Sybil Smith, ed. *Parish Nursing: A Handbook for the New Millennium* (New York: Haworth Pastoral Press, 2003), 166.

7. Jackson Carroll, "Leadership and the Study of the Congregation," in Nancy Ammerman, Jackson Carroll, Carl Dudley, and William McKinney, ed. *Studying Congregations* (Nashville: Abingdon Press, 1998), 190.

8. Fuentes, "Program Evaluation," 176.

9. "Health Ministry Self Study for Congregations," available online at http://www.wheatridge.org (accessed June 19, 2004).

10. Mary Ann McDermott, "Accountability," in Phyllis Ann Solari-Twadell and Mary Ann McDermott, eds., *Parish Nursing: Promoting Whole Person Health Within Faith Communities* (Thousand Oaks, Cal.: Sage, 1999), 228–29.

11. The standards of parish nursing are available either through the Health Ministries Association, 800-280-9919, http://www.hmassoc .org, or the American Nurses Association, 800-637-0323, http://www .nursingworld.org.

CHAPTER TEN

1. Alvene Rethemeyer and Barbara Wehling, "How are we Doing? Measuring Effectiveness of Parish Nursing," *Journal of Christian Nursing* (Spring 2004): 10.

2. For more information on North Park Theological Seminary's faith and health program, see http://www.northpark.edu/sem.

3. Abigail Rian Evans, "Healthy Living, Wholly Lives; Achieving Health at Seminary," *Princeton Seminary Bulletin* (2000): 324–42.

4. Gwen Wagstrom Halaas, *Ministerial Health and Wellness Report, 2002 Evangelical Lutheran Church in America Executive Summary* (Chicago: Evangelical Lutheran Church of America, 2002), 25–27.

5. David Carlson, "Roots and Visions for Health Ministry" (June 2003), available online at http://www.hmassoc.org, 2.

6. Ibid., 6–7.

7. Phone conversation with Susan Fuentes, vice president and director of the Queens Care Health and Faith Partnership, April 16, 2004.

8. Tim Sandquist, "Sports Ministry," presentation at Covenant Midwinter Conference, Rosemont, Illinois, February 5, 2004.

9. I am indebted to Rev. Jackie Bellile for her thoughts on integrating health in a new church plant.